The Translator and Editor

SHEILA MURNAGHAN is the Alfred Reginald Allen Memorial Professor of Greek at the University of Pennsylvania. She is the author of *Disguise and Recognition in the Odyssey* and numerous articles on Greek epic and tragedy, gender in classical culture, and classical reception, and the coauthor of *Childhood and the Classics: Britain and America, 1850–1965*. She is the translator and editor of Euripides' *Medea: A Norton Critical Edition* and the coeditor of *Odyssean Identities in Modern Cultures: The Journey Home*, *Women and Slaves in Greco-Roman Culture: Differential Equations*, and *Hip Sublime: Beat Writers and the Classical Tradition*.

NORTON CRITICAL EDITIONS
Ancient, Classical, and Medieval Eras

For a complete list of Norton Critical Editions, visit
wwnorton.com/nortoncriticals

A NORTON CRITICAL EDITION

Sophocles
ANTIGONE

A NEW TRANSLATION
CONTEXTS
CRITICISM

Translated and Edited by

SHEILA MURNAGHAN
UNIVERSITY OF PENNSYLVANIA

W. W. NORTON & COMPANY
Celebrating a Century of Independent Publishing

W. W. Norton & Company has been independent since its founding in 1923, when William Warder Norton and Mary D. Herter Norton first published lectures delivered at the People's Institute, the adult education division of New York City's Cooper Union. The firm soon expanded its program beyond the Institute, publishing books by celebrated academics from America and abroad. By midcentury, the two major pillars of Norton's publishing program—trade books and college texts—were firmly established. In the 1950s, the Norton family transferred control of the company to its employees, and today—with a staff of five hundred and hundreds of trade, college, and professional titles published each year—W. W. Norton & Company stands as the largest and oldest publishing house owned wholly by its employees.

Manufacturing by Maple Press
Book design by Antonina Krass
Production manager: Brenda Manzanedo

Library of Congress Cataloging-in-Publication Data

Names: Sophocles, author. | Murnaghan, Sheila, 1951– translator, editor.
Title: Antigone : a new translation, contexts, criticism / Sophocles ; translated
    and edited by Sheila Murnaghan, University of Pennsylvania.
Other titles: Antigone. English
Description: New York, NY : W. W. Norton & Company, Inc., [2023] |
    Series: Norton critical edition | Includes bibliographical references.
Identifiers: LCCN 2022057462 | **ISBN 9780393655186 (paperback)** |
    ISBN 9780393655193 (epub)
Subjects: LCSH: Antigone (Mythological character)—Drama. | Sophocles.
    Antigone. | LCGFT: Drama. | Literary criticism.
Classification: LCC PA4414.A7 M79 2023 | DDC 882/.01—dc23/eng/20230210
LC record available at https://lccn.loc.gov/2022057462

W. W. Norton & Company, Inc., 500 Fifth Avenue, New York, N.Y. 10110
    www.wwnorton.com
W. W. Norton & Company Ltd., 15 Carlisle Street, London W1D 3BS

1 2 3 4 5 6 7 8 9 0

For Victor Bers

Contents

Introduction

The events of *Antigone* come at the end of a multigenerational story of trouble in the family of Oedipus, often referred to as the Theban Legend. In the version told by Sophocles, the Theban ruler Oedipus makes the shattering discovery that he has inadvertently murdered his father Laius and married his mother Jocasta.[1] As a consequence, Jocasta commits suicide and Oedipus blinds himself, leaves Thebes, and eventually dies in exile. Their two sons, Eteocles and Polyneices (or Polynices), inherit Oedipus' power but are unable to cooperate in sharing it. Eteocles takes control of Thebes while Polyneices makes an alliance with the rival city of Argos, from which he attacks Thebes with an army led by himself and six Argive champions, an episode known as the Seven against Thebes. In the battle that follows, the Thebans repel the invaders and kill the Argive champions, but they lose their leader when Eteocles and Polyneices meet in single combat and each brother kills the other; at this point, Jocasta's brother Creon becomes the new ruler of Thebes.

Most ancient accounts of the Seven against Thebes ended with the Thebans dishonoring the defeated enemy by refusing to allow the Argives to recover the bodies of their dead for proper burial. In a version that was told with particular pride in Athens, the city where *Antigone* was first performed, the Athenians, led by their legendary king Theseus, then fought the Thebans and forced them to give the bodies back. This high-minded intervention, in which the city extended itself to uphold widely recognized religious and cultural obligations to the dead, was dramatized by both Aeschylus and Euripides, the two most prominent Athenian tragedians other than Sophocles, and was a frequent topic of Athenian patriotic rhetoric. One example of this rhetoric is the excerpt from Lysias' Funeral Oration included in the Ancient Contexts section of this volume.

---

1. Oedipus' troubles originate with previous generations of his famously cursed and transgressive family. His grandfather Labdacus, a grandson of Cadmus, the founder of Thebes, died very young. His father Laius abducted and raped his host's son; then, after he married Jocasta, they were warned by an oracle that if they had a son, that son would kill his father; they did so anyway, and when Oedipus was born they had him exposed in the expectation that he would die.

But the authors of tragedies had a lot of freedom to reshape traditional myths, and Sophocles presented his audience with a different version of the conflict over burial that followed the Theban victory. He made the denial of burial apply only to Polyneices, the Theban insider who had attacked his own city. And he made the champion of that burial not another city and its army, but a young woman from within the Theban ruling family, Antigone, the sister of Eteocles and Polyneices and the niece of the new ruler Creon. In this way, he turned a story about intercity relations into one about internal conflicts within a family and a city, and he created a remarkable heroine who has been repeatedly celebrated, puzzled over, and reimagined ever since the play was first produced, probably sometime in the 440s B.C.E.

When Antigone defies Creon's orders that Polyneices' corpse must be left unburied, exposed to the elements and to scavenging animals, this sets off a personal and political crisis affecting all of their closest family members: Antigone's sister Ismene, the only other surviving descendent of Oedipus; Creon's wife Eurydice and their son Haemon, who is both Antigone's cousin and her fiancé. The clash between Antigone and Creon has disastrous consequences for the entire ruling family and exposes potential fault lines that would threaten the success of any community. As the play presents two headstrong individuals responding in the moment to unusually challenging circumstances, it also raises broader issues that spoke to the concerns of its initial audience and have continued to resonate across many subsequent times and places. Antigone and Creon's dispute over the proper treatment of Polyneices becomes the occasion for an individual's resistance to political authority and opens rifts between the interests of city and family, male and female, old and young, the living and the dead, human laws and transcendent principles.

The Tragic City

That Sophocles reworked an uplifting story about Athenian power and success into a spectacle of catastrophic conflict set in Thebes is a reflection of tragedy's distinctive relationship to the community in which it was performed. Tragedy was invented in Athens and was a major source of the city's high cultural prestige throughout the Greek world. As discussed below, tragic performances were organized by city officials and staged during an annual festival in honor of the god Dionysus that was also a self-conscious demonstration of Athenian greatness. But the plays themselves presented violent, sensational scenarios of conflict and social breakdown that challenged the confident vision promoted in patriotic rhetoric of a well-functioning, cohesive community united against external enemies.

These searching portrayals of communities under stress had clear contemporary relevance, but they were also situated at a certain distance from the here-and-now of the original audience. The plays are set in the mythological past, and their most transgressive and terrifying events do not happen in Athens, which generally figures in tragedy as a well-ordered city and a refuge for suffering outsiders, but rather in other cities, especially Thebes, which often serves as a dark mirror or anti-Athens. Ruled by hereditary monarchs, the legendary cities of tragedy have a different political structure than Sophocles' Athens, which had been for many decades a form of direct democracy, with major decisions taken by a citizen assembly and without a single ruler. But even in that democracy, the city was dominated by powerful individuals, often from aristocratic families, whose roles were variously reflected in tragedy's mythological kings. Those kings are sometimes admirable figures, especially when they consult the people and respect their views, as in several versions of the Athenian king Theseus. At other times, they are troublesome autocrats, whose behavior resembles that of the illegitimate tyrants from which the democracy had freed itself, as happens with Creon in *Antigone*.

In the monarchical settings of tragic plots, political power is bound up with family relations: in *Antigone,* Creon has come to power because, as Jocasta's brother, he is the uncle of Oedipus' two dead heirs. This overlap between political and familial interests allows tragedy to foreground concerns and perspectives that were not prominent in contemporary political discourse. Women in particular are far more vocal and visible in tragedy than they were in the public life of Athens, in ways that Mark Griffith explores in more detail in the essay included in the Criticism section of this volume. Athenian women were defined primarily by their roles as wives and mothers, and were legally under the control of a male guardian (a father, husband, brother, or uncle). Their activities were centered on the household, and elite women in particular were expected to lead secluded lives (poorer women were more likely to be working outside the house, for example as midwives or sellers of produce in the marketplace). Women did play certain key roles in shared religious rituals, but they did not participate at all in the city's governance.

In the city's idealized view of itself, women could stay safely out of view, focused on the family and the household, because men were doing their job of running things, and especially of protecting the whole city from outside threats. In one of the most celebrated examples of Athenian patriotic rhetoric—the Funeral Speech that, according to the historian Thucydides, the politician Pericles delivered a few years after the first performance of *Antigone*—soaring praise of the city's cultural and military achievements is followed by the statement that, where the widows of the fallen are concerned, the most honorable course for them is not to do anything that causes them to be spoken about among men, whether for praise or for blame.

In the messier situations depicted in tragedy, however, female characters often step up and take public action, usually when men have failed in their responsibilities. Tragedy is in part a culturally sanctioned version of the kind of speech that Pericles would have liked to see prevented: speech about women that happens among men. The plays were written by men, performed exclusively by men, and aimed primarily at a male audience; whether ancient Greek women even attended the theater is a much-debated question, which cannot be conclusively answered on the available evidence. The imaginary women of tragedy indicate impressive sympathy for the experiences and concerns of women on the part of those male playwrights, and they must have made a significant impact on the men who enacted or witnessed their words and actions. But the treatment of women in tragedy cannot easily be characterized as either praise or blame. The actions taken by tragic women are understandable reactions to the missteps of men, but they can be as transgressive and destructive as the offenses to which they respond, or even more so, and tragedy as a whole offers no simple or unified answers about the nature and proper roles of women. In the case of *Antigone,* the play does not provide clear guidance about how to evaluate Antigone's defiant behavior—or the behavior of the inexperienced male ruler whom she defies.

The Trials of Creon

In the figure of Creon, the audience of *Antigone* is presented with a newly installed leader trying to establish himself. Coming to power in the wake of a threatening military attack, he prioritizes punishment of the city's enemies through his edict against the burial of Polyneices. Creon sees Polyneices not as his nephew, but as a traitor who has threatened the city's survival, for which he is himself responsible. From that perspective, the prohibition of burial is an understandable if harsh response. Sophocles' contemporaries certainly recognized revenge on enemies as a powerful and legitimate motivation. The refusal of burial did not, according to the Greeks, prevent a dead enemy's soul from reaching the underworld, but it was a way of extending the dishonor of his defeat, especially when it involved mutilation of the body by wild animals. In fifth-century B.C.E. Athens, refusal of burial within the city limits was an established punishment for traitors and temple robbers, and criminals could be executed by being thrown over a cliff into a pit, where their bodies would simply be left. For Creon, this measure is a necessary

affirmation of loyalty to the city as a paramount virtue, on which
the well-being of its citizens depends.

> I think a man is completely worthless
> who puts personal ties above his country.
> And may all-seeing Zeus be my witness:
> I could never stay silent if I saw
> our citizens threatened with disaster;
> and I could never choose for a friend
> a man who is hostile to our country. (182–88)

In a speech delivered about a century later, these words are quoted
approvingly by the prominent politician and orator Demosthenes as
he invokes the norms of behavior in public office that he accuses
his opponent of violating (Demosthenes 19.247).

But Creon's normative pronouncements are hardly adequate to his
tricky situation. As he delivers his first public speech, the audience
already knows that Antigone is so offended by his edict that she will
risk her life to defy it. Her defiance springs from important coun-
tervailing considerations that Creon does not acknowledge. Polyneices is not only a disgraced enemy but a member of Antigone's own
family, which is also the royal family of Thebes and Creon's family
too. His death represents a personal loss for these close relatives,
and it imposes on them the obligation to carry out prescribed rites
of mourning and burial. Antigone's instinctive conviction that she
must do what Creon has forbidden answers to that obligation, which
is religious as well as familial, backed not only by human custom
but by the gods.

The divergent perspectives that lead Creon and Antigone to value
Polyneices so differently cause them to talk past one another, and
they often use the same words in significantly different ways, something that is hard to convey in a translation. This is especially the
case with words that share the root *phil-* and variously connote relations of kinship, friendship, personal attachment, and political alliance. In the speech quoted above, Creon uses this terminology for
the person that he would or would not accept "as a friend" (*philon*)
based on his loyalty to the city; but earlier Antigone has used the
adjectival version of this same word when referring to herself and
Polyneices as belonging absolutely to one another: "I am his [*philē*]:
with him I will lie with my own [*philou*]" (73).

A major factor in this division is gender, which plays a significant
and complicating role both in Antigone's decision to act and in
Creon's harsh and ultimately deadly reaction. As a woman, Antigone
has a primary identification with the family rather than the political sphere of civic and military affairs. Throughout ancient Greek
culture, lamentation and care for the dead—especially in the earliest

and most intimate phases, before the public funeral—were the
responsibility of women, who were closely identified with life's end
as well as its beginning in childbirth. Yet, while Antigone can be
seen as a champion of traditional women's values, she also violates
her expected female role by defying male authority, and specifically
her uncle, who is her legal guardian. This contradiction is dramatized in the play's opening scene, where Antigone's sister Ismene sur-
prises and enrages her by maintaining that their lack of power as
women excuses them from the dangerous mission to which Antigone
has committed herself.

When Antigone is caught disobeying Creon's orders and has to
explain herself to him, she aligns the familial and religious obligations that he has disregarded with "the gods' unfailing and unwritten laws" (455), which override any law that a human ruler like Creon
might make. In Pericles' Funeral Speech we see a prominent male
politician using the same formulation to make a similar point: in a
sentence quoted on p. 45 of this volume, he praises the city for honoring just such universal unwritten laws. But when this same
imperative is invoked by a woman who is challenging Creon's
authority, it is impossible for him to see that he could be wrong. To
yield to a woman, a person who should properly be under his control,
would be an unacceptable sign of social breakdown and personal
weakness. When his son Haemon tries to speak up for Antigone,
Creon assumes that Haemon is bewitched by love, diverted from his
natural allegiance to his father by the dangerously seductive powers
that Greek men often attributed to women.

Age is also a factor in Creon's deafness to Haemon: he cannot
accept having his mind changed by someone younger, even his loyal
and beloved son. As a result, Haemon's attempt to persuade him
only makes Creon more defensive and self-assertive. He is unable to
believe Haemon's claim that public sentiment favors Antigone and
assumes that anyone who opposes him must be plotting to take over
his power or has been bribed by his enemies. And so he repudiates
his son and devises an exceptionally cruel punishment for Antigone.

Creon's conviction that others are plotting against him is typical
of the self-regarding paranoia that the Greeks associated with dangerous tyrants. We see him default to this explanation when challenged by something that he cannot accept or understand. After a
nervous guard reports the news that someone has in fact buried the
body, the Chorus of Theban elders raises the possibility that a god
might have been behind this mysterious act. But the thought that a
god could have favored the dead body of someone who in life attacked
his own city is inconceivable to Creon: "You think that the gods
honor bad people? / Well, they don't!" (288–89). He is rudely dismissive of the venerable Chorus members as well as the hapless

guard, and insists that there are men in the city who are resistant to his rule and that these men have bribed the guards to carry out the burial.

Creon only understands how blind he has been with the appearance of Teiresias, the literally blind prophet who specializes in telling unpalatable truths to Theban rulers (as he does as well in Sophocles' play about Oedipus, *Oedipus Tyrannos*). Teiresias reports clear signs of divine displeasure at Creon's treatment both of Polyneices' body and of Antigone and stresses to him the essential point that the dead are owed different treatment than the living: "Let the dead be. Stop kicking a corpse. / What is so brave about killing a dead man?" (1029–30). And even then, Creon only takes Teiresias seriously when the chorus reminds him that the prophet has never been wrong in the past: his first impulse is to assume that Teiresias has been bribed by his enemies. Once Creon accepts that he has offended the gods, the rest of the play focuses on his belated and humbling attempts to reverse his terrible missteps. While he succeeds in giving Polyneices an appropriate funeral, he fails to prevent a cascade of suicides, and the play ends with Creon in a state of overwhelming humiliation and loss. As the essay by Charles Segal included in the Criticism section of this volume explores in detail, he is ultimately caught up in the kind of conspicuous grieving he himself had tried to prohibit.

One source of Creon's blindness is his confidence in his own ability to master and control his environment. This confidence chimes with the more general admiration for human capacities expressed in one of the most stirring and famous choral odes in the play, the song that begins "Many things to marvel at!" (332) and celebrates human achievements in seafaring, agriculture, hunting, statecraft, and medicine. The exhilaration captured in this ode reflects in part the intellectual trends of Sophocles' time. Many leading fifth-century thinkers, often grouped under the label "Sophists," celebrated humans and their many abilities and elevated them over the traditional gods. Sophocles was clearly receptive to the ideas of the Sophists, which are reflected throughout his works, but his plays repeatedly confirm the infinitely greater power of the gods to shape human experience. That power is undeniable, even if the gods' purposes are communicated opaquely, often through enigmatic oracles and prophecies, and sometimes hard to square with a human sense of justice.

In that choral ode, the word used to characterize human beings—*deina*, here translated "to marvel at"—sounds a note of warning as well as of optimism: it can indicate what is frightening and destructive as well as exciting and awe-inspiring. The Chorus also goes on to stipulate that human success must be aligned with reverence for the gods:

> One who honors a country's laws,
> and the justice of its gods,
> rises high with their city.
> But there is no city
> for someone bound on reckless evil. (368–72)

When Creon loses sight of that crucial alignment of human and divine justice, he falls hard, and his defeat is described through metaphors in which humanity's glorious achievements fail or are turned against him. In his opening speech, Creon envisions himself as a skillful helmsman of the city:

> If the ship of state is properly sailed,
> then we are safe and will gain true friends.
> With laws like these, I'll make this city strong. (189–91)

But by the end he has been brought to his knees by the "Foul harbor of Hades" (1284). Similarly, Creon readily describes his dealings with others in terms of the control over animals that the Chorus lists as one of the great human achievements. He describes the men he thinks are plotting against him as those who "won't submit / to the yoke, do what's right, and support me" (291–92). But the independence of the animal world is registered in the disturbing behaviors of birds that Teiresias reports on, and the ultimate effect of Creon's self-assertion is to turn his own beloved son Haemon into an inarticulate, hostile animal:

> His son just looked at him with wild-beast eyes;
> he gave no answer but spat on his father
> and drew his sword. (1231–33)

The Enigma of Antigone

Through Teiresias' revelations, the play provides a clear indication that Creon is wrong to act as he does: his treatment of both Polyneices and Antigone is shown to violate divinely backed norms. But Sophocles' gods are never fully knowable, and there is no corresponding sign of divine approval for Antigone's acts of defiance. The pollution caused by Polyneices' mistreatment proves that she is right that Polyneices has to be buried, and Antigone understandably believes that, as the only surviving members of their family, she and Ismene are the ones who must do it. But her efforts are useless in the face of Creon's power: her two attempts at a makeshift burial do not prevent that pollution, and Polyneices cannot be effectively buried until Creon changes his mind. In defending herself, Antigone expresses a strong conviction that she has acted in accord with the will of the gods, but there is no external sign to confirm this and no divine intervention to prevent her paying the highest price for her actions. When she is faced with this harsh reality, she is shaken and perplexed by the gods' indifference and struggles to understand why she is being allowed to die for pious behavior.

> Alone, in despair, deserted by friends,
> I go, still alive, to the caves of the dead.
> What have I done to offend the gods?
> Why should I even look to the gods?
> Who can I call on? I honored the gods
> and for that I'm convicted of sacrilege.
> If the gods truly think that this is right,
> what I suffer will teach me that I am wrong. (919–26)

This divine silence leaves the question of how Antigone's actions should be judged open to interpretation. Most modern readers see her as the undisputed heroine of the play; her defiance of Creon is often identified with the modern concept of civil disobedience, according to which it is ethically justified, even required, to disobey unjust laws. But we cannot be sure how Sophocles' contemporaries would have viewed her, and we should not assume that they would all have seen her the same way. In the essay included in the Criticism section of this volume, Judith Fletcher makes a strong case that Antigone represents the civic ideals of Sophocles' Athens better than Creon does, but not all critics would agree. Within the play itself, we get only partial and contradictory indications of public opinion about her behavior. Haemon, speaking as her advocate and mindful of Creon's concern for his standing in the community, insists that the Theban people think she should be honored for her actions, even if they are afraid to say so to his face.

> But I pick up what is secretly whispered.
> The city grieves to see that girl facing
> a shameful death that she hardly deserves,
> when she has performed most glorious acts:
> she would not let her own brother be left
> lying unburied in the gore where he fell
> to be eaten up by birds and wild dogs.
> Shouldn't golden honor be her reward?
> Thoughts like these are spreading in the dark. (692–700)

Yet the Theban citizens whose voices are heard directly, the elders who make up the Chorus, have a different perspective. Every tragic playwright had to make a choice about what role to assign to the chorus, the group of singers and dancers who figure in the plot as interested bystanders while they also voice in their songs a more detached and wide-ranging perspective. In *Antigone*, Sophocles chose to make the Chorus a group of elite male citizens with a history of advising and supporting the city's rulers. These men share Creon's orientation to the political health of the city, and they become active in guiding him as his own position becomes shakier, but they are not provoked and threatened by Antigone as he is. They are puzzled and dismayed to see her led in as the culprit who defied Creon's orders, and they speak up to prevent Creon from punishing Ismene as well. When Antigone is being led off to die, they are overcome by sorrow at her fate.

For all their sympathy, however, the Theban elders, like Ismene in the opening scene, are not willing to endorse Antigone's action. As she laments her imminent death, they insist that she is the victim of her own self-willed nature, which they see as a legacy from her father Oedipus, and they remind her that she is being justly punished for breaking the city's laws.

> Stepping past the limits of daring,
> you stumbled, child, on the altar
> of justice. Now you pay a penalty
> passed down from your father. (853–56)

In keeping with their social position, the Chorus here voices strong support for obedience to a community's laws even at the point when Antigone's situation is most poignant and pitiful. This adds to the sense of isolation and abandonment with which she confronts her death, but also affirms that sympathetic and well-meaning observers might still find her punishment warranted.

Even if Antigone is justly punished, which many modern readers of the play would dispute, she can still command the strong sympathy that even these law-respecting Theban elders feel for her. One of the glories of tragedy is its sensitive, insightful portraits of transgressive figures: leaders who threaten their own communities, like Antigone's father/brother Oedipus, or criminal actors like Medea in Euripides' *Medea*, who kills her own children in response to the wrongs she has suffered. In *Antigone*, Sophocles gives a compelling voice to a young woman who would not have been seen or heard under normal conditions and makes her behavior understandable, even though she breaks the law and is not a straightforwardly likable character.

Antigone's difficult nature is highlighted by the contrast with her milder sister Ismene. This emerges at once in the opening episode, where Antigone turns on Ismene with breathtaking speed because Ismene does not immediately fall in with her plan: in less than a hundred lines her dear sister becomes her despised enemy. Antigone reacts to Creon's authoritarian posturing with open insolence, provoking him to yet more extreme reactions. In her confidence in her own rightness and her quickness to take sides, she more closely resembles Creon than any other character in the play: the deadly course of the plot is the joint creation of two exceptionally willful figures who are as alike in temperament as they are different in their social roles and primary allegiances. The Chorus describes Antigone's particularly difficult nature as an inheritance from her father, and it is hard not to see her as being in part shaped by the transgressive closeness of her incestuous family. Her commitment to a tight circle of self-destructive dead relatives is so strong that she can seem unnaturally morbid, as if consumed by a death wish that explains her reckless lack of concern for her own survival.

Antigone is also challenging to interpret because the explanations she gives for her actions are not consistent, but shift and develop as she reacts to various provocations. When she first appears, she seems simply to be motivated by certainty that Polyneices must be buried. In the face of Ismene's opposition, she begins to articulate what it might mean to take on that mission, defining it as an expression of familial love and a noble cause worth sacrificing her life for. It is only when she has to respond to Creon's reminder that she has knowingly violated his edict that she conceptualizes the burial of the dead as obedience to timeless, unwritten divine laws that antedate and supersede all rules made up by humans.

The speech Antigone gives just before she is led off to her punishment has been especially perplexing to readers and critics because she seems to contradict her own earlier appeal to universal principles. She reiterates her conviction that she did the right thing for her brother by proclaiming that she would not have done the same for a husband or a child. The explanation she gives for this claim—that a lost husband or son could be replaced, while, with her parents dead, she could never have another brother—is better suited to the folktale-like anecdote that is likely to have been Sophocles' source, which is included in the Ancient Contexts section of this volume on pp. 46–47. There, a woman has the chance to save one of her existing male relatives from execution and chooses her brother, while Antigone has no husband or son whom she might or might not bury. But that poignant difference is probably also the best explanation for Antigone's strange argument. She distances herself from the roles of wife and mother when she has to face the fact that she will be losing out on those experiences, which in ancient Greece constituted the defining milestones of a woman's life. She responds to her lost future by arguing that those relationships do not matter as much as her tie to her brother. But only a few lines later, she also laments that she is being led away with "no chance of marriage, no wedding song, / no chance of being a wife or a mother" (917–18), giving voice to her growing awareness of what it will really mean for her die. As a dramatist, Sophocles has brilliantly captured the way that people often decide first and explain themselves afterwards, rationalizing their actions differently under different circumstances. But this portrait does not entirely match the expectations of those for whom Antigone is a model of unwavering devotion to fixed principles.

The death of Polyneices, a disruptive figure who is at once Thebes' friend and enemy, a royal insider and the leader of an attacking army, disables the alliances on which the successful functioning of the city depends: between the interests of the city as a political unit and those of the individual families that make it up; between the interests of men in their military and political roles and those of women as sisters, wives, and mothers; between the country's laws and the justice of its gods. The result is a lethal collision between two characters who would not necessarily have clashed under ordinary circumstances.

Creon and Antigone are not advocating for different visions of how a city should be governed, and their values are not as mutually exclusive or polarized as they come to seem. In his very first words, Creon acknowledges the role of the gods in the city's narrow escape, and he later describes successful management of a family as one sign of a good citizen, even if he cannot himself live up to that standard. As Kirk Ormand points out in the essay included in the Criticism section of this volume, he cannot construct a wholly male family, much as he might like to. When Antigone complicates her intense focus on her dead brother by also lamenting her missed opportunities to be a wife and mother, she is acknowledging the ties between families that make up the larger community and provide the city with new generations of citizens. Under better circumstances the two of them might agree on the proper application of words like "friend," "enemy," "law," and "justice" instead of using them in incompatible ways. But under these circumstances, their inflexible responses destroy the Theban royal household and bring to a close that family's multigenerational history of fatal misalignments.

This bleak conclusion raises the question of whether the play leaves us with anything positive, beyond the emotional release that may follow the arousal of negative emotions—that experience of "catharsis" that has been attributed especially to tragedy ever since *The Poetics,* the influential treatise on tragedy by the fourth-century B.C.E. philosopher Aristotle. It may be that for some spectators in democratic Athens the obliteration of a line of rule-breaking hereditary rulers represented a form of progress and so a cause for celebration. But others may have looked up to the glamorous aristocratic families that still played an outsized role in the city, and viewers in all times and of all political convictions can be drawn into sympathy with the struggles of the powerful. The events of *Antigone* might also be seen as instructive for the citizens who were active participants in the city's governance, conveying lessons about the pitfalls of power and the importance of listening to dissenting voices that could be applied in less extreme situations. For those citizens, simply being confronted with issues as difficult as those raised by this play could be valuable preparation for the kinds of debates in which they were expected to take part.

The Afterlife of Antigone

Another possible answer to the question of whether the play has any positive outcome comes from the Chorus, who remind Antigone that even as she is losing her life she is gaining lasting fame—an especially cherished reward in ancient Greek culture. They counter her laments by asking, "But what about the praise and fame / that follow you to death's dark cave?" (817–18). Antigone feels mocked and misunderstood by this question, but the Chorus' prediction has been realized in the extraordinary afterlife of this ancient play and its vivid heroine, a legacy that continues to grow and evolve in our current moment.

In the ancient world, other authors elaborated the story of Antigone in ways that built on but also departed from Sophocles' version. A few decades later, Euripides also wrote a tragedy about her, but he chose to foreground the romantic relationship with Haemon and the roles of wife and mother that Sophocles' Antigone insistently turns her back on; whether this was a deliberate response to Sophocles' version or simply an alternative is impossible to know for sure. Euripides' play itself has not survived, but from the evidence we have (a brief, late summary and a few quotations) it is clear that Haemon was Antigone's accomplice in the burial, that Antigone did not die, and that the two married and had a son. The various versions of the Theban Legend that were developed by Roman writers, especially in the Latin epic *Thebaid*, produced by Statius in the 90s C.E., and in the early modern period, when the influence of Statius and other Roman poets was greater than that of Sophocles, also tend in various ways to heighten the erotic and sentimental possibilities of the story. In Statius' version Antigone's sense of duty to family is accentuated and made both complementary to and competitive with the erotic love of Polyneices' wife Argia, who joins her in the burial. In the medieval romance tradition, Antigone is herself an erotic object, fought over by several rival kings. In the neoclassical tragedy of the

French poet Robert Garnier, *Antigone, ou la Piété* (1580), Antigone's devotion to family becomes a Christian virtue.

But Antigone's exceptional fame really took off in the early nineteenth century, a time of renewed interest in Sophocles, especially among German writers and scholars who envisioned ancient Greece as a precursor and inspiration for the emerging German nation. The play became at this time a touchstone for philosophical thought, beginning with an influential treatment by G. W. F. Hegel in his *Lectures on the Philosophy of Religion*. Hegel's argument is complicated, but central to his interpretation is the idea that Antigone and Creon are both equally right in their devotion to the competing claims of family and state and both equally wrong in their one-sidedness, which true justice must transcend. In the same period, there began to be revivals of Sophocles' original version, sometimes with attempts to replicate the ancient staging, along with new adaptations.

In the rich subsequent history of philosophical treatments, new productions, and dramatic adaptations, the play's ongoing prominence has been due above all to its ability to address political issues. In a cultural climate shaped by the ideas about individual rights and responsibilities that took shape during the European Enlightenment of the seventeenth and eighteenth centuries, and by revolutionary challenges to the legitimacy of particular regimes, Antigone's defiant behavior became charged with new significance. Her action is now most often seen as a form of political dissent, frequently conceptualized as an act of civil disobedience or principled resistance to an illegitimate, authoritarian, or repressive regime. The play's potential as a means of commenting on specific modern political conditions is well illustrated by the famous and influential version by the French playwright Jean Anouilh, which was staged in Paris in February 1994, during the Nazi occupation of France. Anouilh's version is at least as ambiguous as the original: his Antigone is a more domestic and less confident figure than Sophocles' and his Creon is less tyrannical. But the circumstances of the play's production have ensured that it is read as a veiled statement of political sympathies, whether for the German occupiers and French collaborators Creon might stand for or for the French resistance with whom Antigone can be identified.

In the intervening decades, *Antigone* has transcended the European context of its pre-twentieth-century reception and become a global possession, the most frequently performed and rewritten Greek tragedy, embraced above all as an infinitely adaptable expression of political critique. As scholars who study this ever-proliferating phenomenon have pointed out, versions of *Antigone* have clustered especially in times and places of heightened political conflict, such as apartheid-era South Africa, the dictatorships of

late-twentieth-century South and Central America, or Northern
Ireland during the sectarian "Troubles." Some of the best-known
examples include *The Island* by Athol Fugard, John Kani, and Winston Ntshona (first performed in Cape Town in 1973, and excerpted
in this Norton Critical Edition), *Antigona furiosa* by Griselda Gom-
baro (first performed in Buenos Aires in 1986), and *The Burial at
Thebes* by Seamus Heaney (first performed in Dublin in 2004), but
those are just a few out of hundreds of new versions, which reimag-
ine the original play and its underlying myth in relation to a multitude of local histories and performance traditions. Further examples
are discussed in the essays by Helene Foley and Betine van Zyl Smit
included in the Criticism section of this volume.

The ongoing impact of *Antigone* is not confined to new dramatic
stagings with immediate political resonance. The play remains an
authoritative point of reference for the fields of psychology, philosophy, and political science, and a number of thinkers have taken their
bearings from Sophocles' portrayal of Antigone's challenging person-
ality and unorthodox circumstances. For the French psychologist
Jacques Lacan, her willingness to die is the starting point for an
account of the desire for death as a drive that surpasses ordinary
human rules and categories of evaluation. For the American philosopher of gender and queer theorist Judith Butler, Antigone's status
as the product of incest and her extreme, quasi-incestuous attachment to her brother make her a useful figure through whom to question and rethink traditional models of kinship and normative
sexuality. There are new retellings of Antigone's story in other genres,
such as Kamila Shamsie's 2017 novel *Home Fire,* which recasts
Antigone and her family as British Muslims whose troubles begin when
the Polyneices figure leaves to join ISIS. Yet another recent variation is a distinguished 2011 retelling of *Antigone* for children by the
Scottish novelist Ali Smith, in which she neatly sums up the main
import of the play from a present-day perspective: "what happens
when an individual person stands against the rules and the politics
of the city and country she lives in, or a small powerless girl stands
up to an all-powerful-seeming king, or a single person refuses to
do what a tyrant says she should."[2] This ongoing valorization of
Antigone has been complemented, both in imaginative retellings and
in theoretical elaborations, by a recent upsurge of interest in Ismene
as providing an alternative model of female subjectivity and female
action that is too readily dismissed both by Sophocles' Antigone herself and by the subsequent readers of his play.

---

2. Ali Smith, *The Story of Antigone* (London: Pushkin Children's Books, 2013 [first published in Italian, 2011]), p. 96.

The Staging of Sophocles' Play

The starting point of this vast legacy was a single performance in Athens, possibly in the late 440s B.C.E. This was put on in the Theater of Dionysus, an outdoor space in which the spectators were seated on benches placed on a slope of the Acropolis, the large hill around which the city had grown up. Those spectators looked down at a flat circular floor, the *orchestra,* where the chorus sang and danced. At the far end of the *orchestra* was a raised platform backed by a simple wooden building with a central door, the *skene*; the action took place on this platform, with the *skene* serving as an unseen interior space—in *Antigone* the palace from which members of the royal family appear and to which they return. The play was presented by an all-male cast of citizen amateurs, which included three actors, who played all of the speaking roles. In *Antigone,* that most likely meant that one actor played Creon, which is the largest role in the play, and another actor played all of Creon's challengers—Antigone, Haemon, Teiresias, and Eurydice—while the third played Ismene, the Guard, and the Messenger. The first two actors not only spoke but also sang, when representing Antigone or Creon at moments of emotional intensity. There were also fifteen chorus members, who sang and danced the choral odes. The performers wore impressive exotic costumes, boots that elevated their height, and masks appropriate to their roles.

Tragedies were staged once a year during a major festival in honor of Dionysus, a god associated especially with wine, revelry, and mystical transformation. Dionysus had a particular connection with the theater, and it is possible that the earliest tragedies were especially focused on his mythology. Even in the examples we have, which come from later stages of the genre's development, Dionysus' powers—at once unsettling and restorative—are often invoked, especially in plays set in Thebes, where he was born. In *Antigone,* the Chorus calls on Dionysus to come to the aid of his native city in their final ode, performed at the pivotal moment when Creon has finally seen the truth and gone off to correct his terrible missteps. The Dionysian festival, or Dionysia, was also a political event, arranged by the city and designed to put the power of Athens on display both for its citizens and for the many visitors who attended it. It took place in March, at the beginning of the sailing season, when many foreigners were present, and the ceremonies preceding the performances included patriotic events such as a parade of war orphans who were raised at the city's expense. By the time of *Antigone,* those ceremonies also included displays of tribute paid to Athens by allied cities.

A central feature of the Dionysia was a series of poetic performances, through which the Athenians both honored their gods and
advertised their cultural achievements. These took the form of competitions that featured both tragedy, a spectacular dramatic form
that had developed in Athens beginning in the late sixth century, and
the dithyramb, one of the nondramatic forms of choral song-and-
dance out of which tragedy had evolved. Each year three playwrights
were selected by city officials to compete with a set of three tragedies and a satyr play, an irreverent, high-spirited mythological bur-
lesque; this meant not only writing the scripts that are the only
aspects of these plays which—in a few surviving examples—are
available to us, but also composing the music and choreography
for the choral odes and training the performers. In most cases, the
plays offered for the competition were unconnected, although
another major tragedian, Aeschylus, did make a practice of turning his three tragedies into coherent trilogies. At the end of the
festival, the three playwrights' entries were ranked and prizes were
awarded for each place. Sophocles won more victories than any
other playwright in these competitions, in which he took part for
roughly six decades, from his first entry in 468 until his death. During that time, he produced over 120 plays, of which only seven now
survive. He came first at the Dionysia eighteen times and was never
placed lower than second; he also did well in competitions at other
festivals.

Antigone is generally dated to about 442 B.C.E. on the basis of the
kind of scrappy evidence on which much of our knowledge of Greek
literary history rests: a summary of the play that was attached to it
several centuries later includes the statement that, as a result of the
success of *Antigone,* Sophocles was chosen to be one of the city's
ten elected generals during an expedition against the island of
Samos that began in 441–40. While the posited cause-and-effect
is questionable, this story would not have circulated unless that
was roughly when the play was produced, and it does tells us something about both the cultural prestige of tragedy and Sophocles'
high standing in Athenian life.

Sophocles was born around 496 B.C.E. into a wealthy family (his
father may have been an arms manufacturer) and died in 406 or 405
after a long and exceptionally successful life. His lifetime coincided
with a period when Athens experienced increasing prosperity and
cultural prominence within the network of independent city-states
that made up the classical Greek world. In the early decades of the
fifth century B.C.E., Athens took the lead in uniting some but not all
of those cities (Thebes was a notable exception) in an alliance to
ward off an invasion from the Persians, who controlled an extensive

empire to the east. After the defeat of the Persians in 479, Athens continued to expand as a naval and sea-trading power, especially under the charismatic leadership of Pericles, and turned the alliance formed to fight the Persians into an extensive power base that was itself a kind of empire. The result was growing tension between Athens and other major cities such as Corinth, Thebes, and Sparta, and ultimately an outright war between Athens and its allies and Sparta and its allies, known as the Peloponnesian or Atheno-Peloponnesian War; this broke out in 431 and lasted until Athens was defeated in 404. The defeat of Athens was a demoralizing blow for the city, but by no means the end of its importance as an intellectual and political center.

Sophocles was an important player in Athenian military and political affairs. He was elected to several prominent offices, including not only the generalship in the Samian war but also positions as a state treasurer and as a member of a special commission set up to deal with a disastrous setback during the Peloponnesian War. He also played a role in the city's religious life, and there was a tradition that when a new cult of the healing god Aesclepius was introduced he kept the god in his house, in the form of a snake, until a proper temple had been built. If the kinds of anecdotes that pass for biographical information in the ancient record can be believed, he was a genial, even-tempered, and pleasure-loving person, and it appears that he was friends with many other literary figures, including the historian Herodotus. In sum, he seems to have enjoyed all the honors, privileges, and pleasures available to the most elite members of his society. Much as the social world of tragedy inverts the upbeat picture painted in patriotic rhetoric, Sophocles' successful life offers a striking contrast with his plays, which spotlight characters who cannot fit in and get along with others, often powerful figures who become outcasts because of their intolerable actions and difficult natures.

Sophocles' surviving works include two other plays about the family of Oedipus, both of which involve an earlier stage of the story than *Antigone* but were composed later: *Oedipus Tyrannos,* which dramatizes Oedipus' discovery of his patricide and incest, and *Oedipus at Colonus,* which dramatizes his death at Athens after many years in exile. While the three plays are often grouped together and labeled "the Theban plays," they were written decades apart and do not form a connected trilogy. Nonetheless, the two Oedipus plays do reflect the earlier *Antigone:* they give attention to Antigone and Ismene and look ahead to the subsequent events dramatized there. In this way, Sophocles himself can be said to be the first in the long list of authors influenced by his *Antigone.*

Oedipus Tyrannos, which may have been written in the 420s, ends with Oedipus saying goodbye to his daughters, now also known to be his sisters, and entrusting them to Creon as he prepares to leave the city. *Oedipus at Colonus* was Sophocles' last play, produced posthumously by his grandson in 401, and represents his final return to the Theban Legend. The play about Antigone that he had written decades earlier was clearly in his mind (this is also reflected in a tradition that he was reciting lines from *Antigone* when he died). In *Oedipus at Colonus,* Sophocles goes out of his way to create a fuller context for the earlier play. He tells a new story about Oedipus' death, which in *Antigone* Ismene recalls as a traumatic event accompanied by disgrace. In this version, after years of wandering with the support of his daughters, Oedipus is welcomed in Athens, where his life comes to a mysterious, peaceful end, and his burial there conveys a permanent benefit on the city.

While in Athens, Oedipus is visited by Polyneices, who wants his father's blessing for his upcoming attack on Thebes. He receives a cold answer: angry at both brothers for excluding him from Thebes because of his criminal past, Oedipus curses them both, assuring their mutual destruction. Before Polyneices leaves, he appeals to Antigone and Ismene:

> If these our father's curses are fulfilled,
> and you somehow come home to Thebes,
> do not deprive me, by the gods, of honor,
> but place me in a tomb with proper rites.
> The praise you earn for doing this will match
> the praise you have now earned for helping him.
> (*Oedipus at Colonus,* 1407–13)[3]

Antigone makes no response to this request and tries instead to talk him out of his attack on Thebes, but Sophocles has prepared the way for her action in *Antigone* and clarified what is left tantalizingly open in the earlier play, where Antigone's certainty about the value of her action and its importance to Polyneices rests solely on her own conviction. At the end of *Oedipus at Colonus,* the sisters make plans to return to Thebes, still hoping to forestall the slaughter that is destined for their brothers. And so, at the very end of his final work, Sophocles once again launches Antigone on her singular, heartbreaking, and glorious career, which continues even now.

---

3. Translated by the editor for the forthcoming Norton Critical Edition of *Oedipus at Colonus.*

A Note on the Translation

As the eminent Sophocles scholar Bernard Knox once pointed out, "the problems facing a translator of Greek tragedy are . . . especially formidable when the poet is Sophocles. His dramatic style, pitched midway between the opulence of Aeschylean imagery and the comparative sobriety of Euripidean rhetoric, can conjure out of highly formal language the illusion of passionate, unpremeditated speech. . . ."[1] I have made it a priority to convey the emotional impact of this text—originally written as a script for live performance—by making Sophocles' characters sound like real people, saying things that real English-speakers might say, even when that means departing further from the exact wording of the Greek than some translators would. But I have also tried to capture the way that Sophocles' speakers communicate their strong feelings through, not despite, the formality of their language, which is marked by regular metrical lines, dignified diction, concision, abstraction, recurrent metaphors, unusual expressions, and simple words charged with heightened meaning. This is a hard balancing act, and any attempt to do justice to Sophocles' dense and freighted language runs the risk of burying rather than unleashing the feelings expressed. In the end, I have often found it better to let go, to accept the limits of what any translation can do, and to look for chances to compensate in one place for what is necessarily lost in another.

This challenge comes up right away with the play's famously difficult first line.[2] Antigone calls out to her sister Ismene in strange and striking terms that reveal her deep investment in their relationship and her expectation that her sister will see things exactly as she does: *ō koinon autadelphon Ismēnēs kara!* A closely literal translation, which might read, "o shared, self-siblinged head of Ismene," is out of the question. The usual solutions involve terms like "dear,"

---

1. Bernard Knox, *Word and Action: Essays on the Ancient Theater* (Baltimore: Johns Hopkins UP, 1979), p. 199.
2. For this and other challenges involved in translating *Antigone*, and the many solutions that have been tried, see Deborah H. Roberts, "Reading *Antigone* in Translation: Text, Paratext, Intertext," in S. E. Wilmer and Audronė Žukauskaitė, eds., *Interrogating Antigone in Postmodern Philosophy and Criticism* (Oxford: Oxford UP, 2010), pp. 283–312. The various translations quoted in the essays in the Criticism section give a taste of other current approaches.

"dearest," and "my own" to express the closeness of the bond, and
"heart," "blood," and "flesh" to reflect the genetic link between the
siblings and the reference to the body in the circumlocution "head
of Ismene." But Antigone's language is abstract and elevated as well
as insistent, and those English words feel too stagy and unidiomatic
to me. So I went for a more abstract expression of how Antigone sees
the relationship: "Ismene, my sister, my second self!" While "second
self" here allows me to echo the first element of the compound *autadelphon*, "self-siblinged," it also mutes an essential feature of the original. "Self-siblinged" or "having the selfsame two parents," here and
elsewhere in the play, evokes the overly close birth relations of the
family of Oedipus, in which a wife is also a mother, daughters are
also sisters, and sons are also brothers. But I was able at least to
hint at the sisters' disturbing origins in the next line. When Antigone
reminds Ismene of their shared evils, which come "from Oedipus,"
I made those be evils "born from Oedipus."

A further challenge arises from the way that Sophocles has built
into his play one of the principal limitations of translation: the fact
that no substituted word or phrase can contain all the meanings of
the original. As they give voice to their conflicting visions, Creon
and Antigone use the same words but mean different things by them.
This is particularly true of two simple, widely used, and flexible
Greek terms. One is *philos*, an adjective and related set of nouns that
designates what is loved, loving, close, or one's own; it can apply to
family members, lovers, friends, chosen companions, loyal support-
ers, and political allies, and also to someone's preferred tastes, activities, and modes of behavior. The question of whether this word
can be used of Polyneices is at the heart of the conflict between
Antigone and Creon. The other term is *nomos*, a noun that often refers
to a formal law but can also indicate a wide range of customs, practices, and social expectations that are understood to be in some way
normative or binding. Given the contested status of Creon's prohibition of Polyneices' burial, whether that should or should not be
designated a *nomos*, and what other rules or principles merit that
label, are major points of contention, as Judith Fletcher discusses
in the essay included in the Criticism section of this volume.

The reader of the Greek text who finds Antigone and Creon using
these value-laden terms in different senses experiences a pointed
reminder of how committed they are to incompatible visions. But
an English translation that aims at an impression of natural speech
cannot always replicate that experience. Antigone introduces the
thematically central language of friendship and enmity in the question she asks Ismene at the end of her first speech, which I translate,
"Or have you missed / enemies' evils descending on friends?" (9–10).

Her words are abstract and ambiguous (are these evils that come from enemies or evils that are suitable only for enemies?), and Ismene is understandably puzzled by them. But as the sisters begin to speak more specifically about their situation, "friend" no longer works for the close relationships they have in mind. Although the same Greek word, *philos*, is being used, I have Ismene answer that she has heard nothing about "the ones we love" (12), and when Antigone declares a little later that she would gladly join Polyneices in death, I have her describe herself as "his" and her brother as "my own" (73). At the end of this conversation, Ismene uses forms of *philos* to sum up her view of her sister: she tells her she is deeply misguided, but nonetheless "*tois philois . . . philē*," herself having the quality of being *philos* in relation to others who are *philos*. I needed a whole line to try to convey the multiple implications of this rich but simple word: "but truly loved and true to those you love" (99).

Later, when Antigone distances herself from Creon's position that a traitor like Polyneices must always be an enemy, whether dead or alive, I have her use the language of friendship and enmity again: "I like to have friends, not enemies" (523). Sophocles has invented new compound verbs for this forceful declaration. More literally, she says, "I have a nature not *sunechthein* [to join in hating/being an enemy] but *sumphilein* [to join in loving/being a friend]." I chose this translation because I wanted her to pick up explicitly on Creon's reference to an "enemy" and because the English language of loving risks being too tame and sentimental in Antigone's case. Her love is disturbingly intense and restrictive and does not rule out hatred: despite what she says, she treats both Creon and Ismene as enemies.

In the case of *nomos*, I have tried to be stricter in following the Greek, although not completely so, and especially to maintain key distinctions where the central issue of the legitimacy of Creon's prohibition is concerned. Creon refers to this as a *nomos*, but Antigone never does. She denies it any connotation of legitimacy by using instead the word *kērugma*, literally "something announced" (which captures Creon's sense that something is automatically right if he says it), which I translate "proclamation." This preserves a telling contrast with Antigone's use of a closely related term to *nomos*, *nomima*, for the "the gods' unfailing and unwritten laws" (455) and of *nomos* for the "law" that explains why she would only have done what she did for a brother and not for a husband or child. And when she applies *nomos* in the sense of "custom" or "norm" to burial rites, I incorporate the language of law to signal that she is using the same term for those rites that she withholds from Creon's proclamation. I have her describe the honors with which Eteocles will be buried with the somewhat strained and overlegal "lawful custom" (24); and when she explains that Hades desires burial even for a traitor, I have her make a point of her usage: "In Hades these rites have the force of law" (519).

In grappling with one of the best-known and most eloquent passages of the play, I found myself dealing with another tricky problem, namely that seemingly straightforward English equivalents can develop distracting new valences over time. The passage in question is the opening of the song that the Chorus sings after they hear of the mysterious burial of Polyneices, in which they evoke the exhilarating range and sobering limitations of human achievement. I am conscious that my version, "Many things to marvel at! / None more than human beings" (332–33), underplays the grandeur and subtlety of the original. "To marvel at" translates the multivalent adjective *deinos*, which can mean "wonderful," "marvelous, "impressive," "formidable," but also "terrible," "frightening," and "sinister." The more positive meaning seems to be uppermost here, but the darker meaning also lurks beneath the surface and becomes more salient as the ode progresses. Some translators convey this ambiguity by using several different English words—for example, "Many wonders, many terrors, / But none more wonderful than the human race / Or more dangerous"[3]—but that has the clear downside of wordiness, as well as a didactic feel (informing the reader of what the Greek professor knows). I wanted to go in the other direction, cutting down on words to keep the English fresh and energetic, in part because the line is already so weighed down by its fame. The single English word that to my mind might best convey the glory and terror combined in *deinos* is "awesome," but that is ruled out by its present-day currency as a casual term of hyperbolic praise.

The Greek word that I translate with the admittedly clunky "human beings," *anthrōpos*, means "man" in the sense of "human being" rather than "male person." "Man" or "mankind" are more obvious and elegant one-word equivalents, and they show up in almost all existing English versions, but those words are no longer viable as a way of referring to the whole of humanity. Sophocles and other members of his society (as well as most modern people until recently) may have been comfortable with a masculine term as the unmarked and normative referent for all people, but that cannot stand in a translation that speaks to a twenty-first-century audience, especially not in a play that reveals the limits of the normative and that has inspired a long tradition of feminist thought and action. "Human race" has been a serviceable alternative for translators who are sensitive to this issue, but that too has become problematic, as

3. Paul Woodruff, trans., *Antigone* (Indianapolis and Cambridge, MA: Hackett Publishing Co., 2001), p. 14.

the fraudulence and malevolence of the concept of race are increasingly recognized. Similarly, thanks to the attentive eye of a student reader, I ended up revising passages in which I had used "savage" when speakers characterize Antigone as turbulent and unruly.

Among the factors that make the language of Sophocles formal is the fact that his characters are always speaking in verse. This is the case even in the dialogue sections, which would have been spoken by the actors, as well as the lyric passages, which would have been sung by the Chorus (while also dancing) or by actors at times of high emotion. The meter used for the dialogue is iambic trimeter, a sequence of six feet in the shape of an iamb (a short syllable followed by a long one in the quantity-based meters of ancient Greek, an unstressed syllable followed by a stressed one in the stress-based meters of English), which was thought to be especially close to ordinary speech. For English translators who use a regular meter, blank verse, or unrhymed iambic pentameter (a sequence of five iambic feet), is generally favored as the closest equivalent. I do not myself fully adopt this meter, but I do aim for lines of roughly ten syllables with a strong iambic element. I also follow the lines of the original Greek text as closely as possible and try to give each line integrity as a unit, something at which Sophocles is particularly adept. I set the lyric passages apart by using shorter lines, sometimes rhythmical, sometimes free verse.

This translation is based on the text by Mark Griffith for the Cambridge Greek and Latin Series and informed throughout by the superb commentary that accompanies it.

Acknowledgments

I am grateful to the two Norton editors who made this edition possible, Carol Bemis, who first invited me to take on *Antigone*, and Rachel Goodman, who has overseen its progress with patience and good humor, offering perceptive comments and expert advice on all aspects of the project. I also thank the friends, students, and fellow translators whose attentive reading of earlier drafts helped to make this translation better, including Jane Gordon, Jeremy Lefkowitz, Annie Ma, Ellen McLaughlin, Deborah H. Roberts, and Emily Wilson. The framing and argumentation of the Introduction were also improved by many excellent suggestions from Jane Gordon and Annie Ma. This work builds on years of trying to grasp the ancient Greek language and ancient Athenian culture, with the help of many teachers. I am pleased to dedicate it to one of my first and most entertaining teachers of Greek, subsequently an exceptionally supportive colleague and loyal friend, Victor Bers, a scholar with a deep understanding of Sophocles and of Greek poetic style.

The Text of
ANTIGONE

Antigone

Cast of characters

Antigone, *daughter of Oedipus and Jocasta*
Ismene, *daughter of Oedipus and Jocasta*
Creon, *ruler of Thebes, uncle of Antigone and Ismene*
Guard, *assigned to watch the corpse of Polyneices*
Haemon, *son of Creon*
Teiresias, *a blind prophet*
Messenger, *one of Creon's attendants*
Eurydice, *wife of Creon, mother of Haemon*

Chorus of Theban elders
Nonspeaking guards and attendants

Setting: in front of the royal palace of Thebes
     Enter ANTIGONE *and* ISMENE.

ANTIGONE
  Ismene, my sister, my second self!
  Is there any evil born from Oedipus
  that Zeus[1] won't make us both live through?
  I see no form of grief or disaster,
  no disgrace, no dishonor, which is not   5
  among the evils that you and I face.
  And what about this new proclamation
  they say our commander's made for the city?
  Have you heard any news? Or have you missed
  enemies' evils descending on friends?   10

ISMENE
  I have had no word, either good or bad,
  of the ones we love since that moment when
  we lost both our brothers, both of them killed
  on a single day with a double blow.

---

1. Principal Olympian god and most powerful authority in the ancient Greek pantheon.

I know the Argive army[2] left last night,   15
but I have heard nothing else since then
that would make things better or worse for me.

ANTIGONE

That's what I thought. And so I brought you here
outside the gates where we can talk alone.

ISMENE

What about? Something has clearly upset you.   20

ANTIGONE

Isn't Creon planning to grant one brother
rites of burial and deprive the other?
Eteocles he hides under the earth,
choosing to follow lawful custom,
so he can be honored among the dead.   25
But Polyneices' miserable corpse—
all who live in Thebes are enjoined, I've heard,
not to cover or mourn, but to leave it there
unwept and unburied, a lucky find
for birds looking out for something to eat.   30
That's what the noble Creon has proclaimed
for you—and me, yes me! And he himself
will be here soon to announce all this
to those who haven't heard; he'll make it clear
that this is no small matter. The penalty   35
that's been prescribed is death by public stoning.
That's how things stand. So now we will see
whether you live up to your noble birth.

ISMENE

You take it so hard! In this situation,
what could I do to make any difference?   40

ANTIGONE

Think about working together with me.

ISMENE

On what sort of venture? What do you mean?

ANTIGONE

You could give me a hand lifting the body.

ISMENE

You plan to bury him? But that's not allowed.

ANTIGONE

I won't abandon him. He is my brother—   45
yours too, though you don't want to do your part.

2. Soldiers from the city of Argos, recruited by Polyneices to attack Thebes. See Introduction, p. ix.

ISMENE
You have to do this, when Creon forbids it?

ANTIGONE
He has no right to keep me from my own.

ISMENE
O sister, think what we have been through;
how our father died despised and disgraced,   *Dad dies* 50
stabbing his own eyes with his own hand,
for the awful things he found he had done;
and our mother, his mother too—and wife   *???*
taking her own life with knotted ropes;
then our two brothers on a single day,   55
bringing a selfsame death on themselves,   *mom kills brothers*
each raising his hand against the other.
Now you and I have been left on our own;
we face a terrible death if we act
against the law and the king's decision.   60
You have to remember that we are women,
not suited by nature to fight against men,
properly ruled by those who are stronger:
we have to accept such things—and still worse.
I will ask the dead for their forgiveness   65
on the grounds that I am under constraint,
but I will submit to those in control.
There is no sense in pointless efforts.

ANTIGONE
Then I won't ask you to get involved.
If you agreed now, I wouldn't want you.   70
Be however you like. I will bury him.
What a fine thing for me to die for that!
I am his: with him I will lie with my own.
My crime is holy, for I have to please
the dead far longer than the living: 75
I will lie with them forever. Feel free
to dishonor what the gods honor most.

ISMENE
I am not dishonoring anything: *> like socrates*
There is no way I could defy the city.   *and crito fight?*

ANTIGONE
That may be good enough for you, but I   80
will make a grave for my beloved brother.

ISMENE
You ask for trouble. You terrify me.

ANTIGONE
Don't worry about me. Look out for yourself.

ISMENE
   Well, don't tell anyone about your plan.
   Just keep it a secret, and I will too.   85
ANTIGONE
   Oh, spread the news! I will hate you more
   if you keep quiet than if you tell the world.
ISMENE
   You have a hot heart for chilling acts.
ANTIGONE
   I will please the people who matter most.
ISMENE
   If you can—but what you crave can't be done.   90
ANTIGONE
   So, when my strength gives out, that's when I'll stop.
ISMENE
   It is not good to chase what can't be done.
ANTIGONE
   If you think that, I really will hate you,
   and our dead brother should hate you too.
   Leave me to my bad plans and dreadful fate.   95
   There is no amount of suffering
   that can keep me from an honorable death.
ISMENE
   Go if you have to. You are out of your mind,
   but truly loved and true to those you love.

      Exit ANTIGONE *and* ISMENE. *Enter the* CHORUS.

CHORUS
   Brilliant ray of golden sun,   100
   loveliest light that ever shone
   on our city's seven gates,
   you appeared to us at last,
   dazzling eye of day!
   Rising over Dirce's[3] streams   105
   you turned back the glinting shields
   of the men who came from Argos.
   They rushed off in headlong flight,
   jolted by your piercing bit.

   Polyneices brought them here,   110
   raising strife on either side.
   Like gleaming eagles, they swooped in,
   shrieking out their bitter cry,
   wings spread wide to block the light,

3. One of the rivers of Thebes.

charging with their countless weapons,   115
and their helmets thick with plumes.

They hovered high above the town,
gaping down with open jaws,
circling the gates with deadly spears,
but fled before they filled their throats,   120
with rich streams of Theban blood,
before the pine-pitch flames of torches
could bring our crown of towers down.
In the din of battle, they went off
forced back by the hard-won triumph   125
of the snake that rose against them.

Zeus hates the sound of boasting tongues:
he saw the invaders pouring in,
a swollen stream of fighting men,
exulting in the clang of gold.   130
He flung down his fiery bolt
against the one who scaled the walls
and shouted victory from the heights.[4]

He staggered and fell to stony ground,
his blazing torch still in his hand,   135
after he'd launched his crazed attack,
with raging hate in every breath.
It did not end as he had hoped.
The others also came to grief:
mighty Ares[5] struck them down,
the lead horse of our team.   140[6]

Seven spearmen at our seven gates,
stationed as equals for an equal fight,
left their weapons as trophies to Zeus.
Except that those two wretched brothers,
born from the selfsame father and mother,   145
planted their spears in one another
as they won a double death.

4. One of the invaders, Capaneus, was notorious for his outrageous boasts and attempts to climb the walls and set the city on fire.
5. Olympian god of war.
6. The lines of lyric passages are divided differently in different editions, but the conventional numbering is retained, which leads at times to inexact line counts.

But now glorious Victory[7]
comes to chariot-driving Thebes.
We will put away the pain   150
of the war that has just ended.
We will visit all the temples
with our night-long dancing.
Let Dionysus[8] lead the way,
lord of whirling revelry.
    Enter CREON.
But wait, here comes our new king.   155
Creon, Menoetius' son, the one
the gods have just now put in place.
What new plan is he mulling over?
Why has he issued a general call
to convene a meeting   160
of the city's elders?

CREON
Friends! After tossing us on stormy seas,
the gods have righted our city once again.
I have summoned you apart from the rest
because I know you respected Laius   165
when he was in power and held the throne,
Oedipus too when he was in charge;
and once he had died, you stood by his sons,
supporting them with your good advice.
Now that those two have met their common fate,   170
dying in tandem, both striking and struck
with kindred bloodshed's polluting blow,
I am in power and I hold the throne
as next of kin to the ones who died.
There's no good way to know a man's nature—   175
his spirit, his judgment, his cast of mind—
until he has been tested as a ruler.
In my view, someone who steers the city
but fails to champion the best ideas,
keeping his mouth shut because he's afraid,   180
has always been the worst kind of leader.
And I think a man's completely worthless
if he puts a friend ahead of his country.
And may all-seeing Zeus be my witness:
I could never stay silent if I saw   185

---

7. In Greek Nikē, personified goddess of victory.
8. Dionysus, god of wine, revelry, magical transformation, and theater, with a close relationship to Thebes, where he was born.

our citizens threatened with disaster;
and I could never choose for a friend
a man who is hostile to our country.
If the ship of state is properly sailed,
then we are safe and will gain true friends.   190
With laws like these, I'll make this city strong.
So I've proclaimed to all who live here
as follows concerning Oedipus' sons:
Eteocles, who died for this city,
fighting for it with the utmost valor,   195
should be placed in a tomb with every rite
that honors the noblest of the dead.
But his blood brother—Polyneices,
who came back from exile with the intent
of burning his own city to the ground   200
with his family's gods, and who also planned
to drink his people's blood and make us slaves—9
no one in this city, it is proclaimed,
should place him in a tomb or mourn for him.
He must stay unburied, his body left out   205
for the birds and dogs, in open disgrace.
That is my thinking. Where I have a say,
traitors will not get more honor than good men.
But whoever wants what's best for this city
will be honored by me, dead or alive.   210

CHORUS
Creon, so that is how you choose to treat
the city's enemy and the city's friend.
Well, you can decide what law to apply
when it comes to the dead, or us the living.

CREON
Then you must see that my words are followed.   215

CHORUS
Ask someone younger to take on that job.

CREON
There are men in place who will guard the corpse.

CHORUS
Then what more are you telling us to do?

CREON
Not to side with any who disobey.

CHORUS
No one's so foolish that he wants to die.   220

---

9. In ancient Greece, where slavery was not based on race, some people were born into
   slavery, but others were enslaved as a result of being defeated in war.

CREON

That *is* the price. But there are many men
who have been ruined by the hope of gain.
          Enter the GUARD.

GUARD

Sir, I won't pretend to be out of breath
from rushing here on eager feet.
Fear kept making me stop in my tracks,   225
always thinking I should just turn around.
A voice in my head kept nagging at me:
"Why go where you're sure to be punished?"
"Oh, you're stopping then? If somebody else
tells Creon the news, won't you be in trouble?"   230
With thoughts like those I dragged out the journey,
turning a short road into a long one.
But I knew I had to come here at last
and say what I know, important or not.
So here I am. I keep telling myself   235
that whatever has to happen will happen.

CREON

And what is it that has you so worried?

GUARD

First I need to explain about myself.
I didn't do it and didn't see who did.
There is no way I should be punished.   240

CREON

Well, you are putting up quite a blockade,
but you clearly have some news to report.

GUARD

Difficult subjects make people nervous.

CREON

Oh just come out with it—and then be gone.

GUARD

Right! That body—someone has buried it.   245
They sprinkled it with thirsty dust, and then,
with the proper rites done, they went away.

CREON

What? Say more. What man dared to do this?

GUARD

No idea. There's no sign of anyone
pounding with an axe or digging up dirt,   250
just the hard, dry ground, not dented by wheels.
Whoever it was did not leave a trace.
When the man on first watch pointed it out
we all of us had a nasty surprise.

The body had vanished—not in a tomb,   255
but covered over with a layer of dust,
just thick enough to avoid pollution.
No dog or wild beast had defaced the corpse.
A lot of harsh words flew back and forth;
each guard accused another. We came close   260
to a fistfight, with no one to stop us.
Any of us could have been the guilty one,
but there was no proof and we all denied it.
We were ready to handle molten lead,
to walk through fire, or to swear any oath   265
that we did not do it and had no clue
who planned this thing or who made it happen.
We were getting nowhere when one of us said
something that made us all very anxious.
We stared at the ground with no good answer   270
and no good plan for warding off trouble.
He pointed out that it was our duty
to tell you this news and not keep quiet.
We had to agree, and so we drew lots.
This lovely task fell to unlucky me.   275
I wish I weren't here—and you feel the same:
bearers of bad news are never welcome.

CHORUS
My lord, I keep coming back to the thought
that somehow a god is behind this act.

CREON
Stop there, before you make me really angry   280
and show that you're foolish as well as old!
What you are saying is out of the question—
that the gods could care about this body.
Do you imagine they covered it over
to honor him like some benefactor?   285
He would have torched their shrines and holy gifts,
and torn up their country and its laws.
You think that the gods honor bad people?
Well, they don't! From the outset some men here
have balked at my rule and muttered against me,   290
secretly shaking their heads. They won't submit
to the yoke, do what's right, and support me.
I am dead certain that these guards were bribed
by those same men to carry out this act.
The silver coin is humans' worst invention.   295
It's the thing that burns cities to the ground
and drives the people out of their houses.

It warps noble minds and teaches them
to turn their thoughts to shameful acts.
It has pointed the way to every crime   300
and every form of godless behavior.
But the ones who took money to do this thing
will find themselves punished sooner or later.
And by Zeus, whom I still hold in honor,
you need to know—for I swear to this—   305
that if you don't find the perpetrator
who did this burial and show him to me,
you will not just be going to Hades:[1]
but strung up alive you will show the cost
of an insolent act, and then you will know   310
where to turn for profit, and you will learn
not to love making everything pay.
Ill-gotten gains are much more likely
to bring people ruin than to keep them safe.

GUARD
May I say something, or should I just go?   315

CREON
Can't you tell that your talking annoys me?

GUARD
Just bothers your ears? Or stings in your mind?

CREON
Why do you need to localize my pain?

GUARD
The one who did it hurts your mind, not me.

CREON
You're clearly someone who just loves to talk!   320

GUARD
But definitely not the perpetrator.

CREON
Oh yes, you are! You sold your soul for gain.

GUARD
Wait![2]
It's not good to judge from what only seems true.

CREON
You can talk about seeming all you want.
But unless you show me who did this thing,   325
you'll know the grief that comes from money-grubbing.

GUARD
Sure, let them be found! But whether they're caught

1. Hades is the name both of the underworld and of the god who presides over it.
2. Brief exclamations such as this are not included in the line count.

or not—and that is really up to chance—
there is no way you'll see me here again.
I did not think I would escape like this.   330
For that, I owe plenty of thanks to the gods.

                    Exit GUARD *and* CREON.

CHORUS
  Many things to marvel at!
  None more than human beings.
  In stormiest winds
  they cross the sea   335
  advancing through
  engulfing waves.
  Earth, the oldest of the gods,
  that never fails and never flags,
  they scrape away at year by year,   340
  plowing her under with their mules.

  The flighty tribe of airborne birds,
  the wild beast clans that roam the land,
  the watery offspring of the sea—
  spreading wide   345
  their knotted nets,
  those clever hunters
  snare them all.
  They tame wild creatures with their tools: 350
  they hold the shaggy stallion in their yoke,
  and the steady mountain bull.

  They taught themselves the art of speech
  and the wind-swift paths of thought,   355
  and the mind that governs cities.
  They have learned the ways to hide
  from frosty air
  and shafts of rain.
  Always ready, they face what comes.   360
  It is only death
  they cannot outwit.
  For the hardest of diseases
  they have figured out the cures.

  With skills that reach   365
  past expectation,
  they sometimes gain and sometimes lose.
  One who honors a country's laws,
  and the justice of its gods,

rises high with their city.   370
But there is no city
for someone bound on reckless evil.
Keep that person from my hearth:
I want no part
of those acts, those thoughts.   375
            Enter the GUARD, *leading* ANTIGONE.
But here's a strange sight.
I can tell who it is, that is not in doubt,
It's that sad girl, Antigone,
unhappy daughter
of unhappy Oedipus.   380
But surely you weren't brought to this place
for breaking the laws imposed by the king,
caught in some nonsense?

GUARD
She is the one who buried the body!
We caught her doing it. So, where's Creon?   385
            Enter CREON.

CHORUS
Here! He's leaving the house just in time.

CREON
What's going on? What am I in time for?

GUARD
Never swear that something can't happen.
A second thought can prove a first one false.
When you stormed at me with your angry threats   390
I vowed not to come back here anytime soon.
But since I've had some unexpected joy—
and there is no greater pleasure than that—
well, now I've come, though I swore I wouldn't.
I bring you this girl: she was caught by us   395
performing the burial. No lots this time!
This is my windfall and it's mine alone.
And now, my lord, you can take her yourself.
Try her, convict her. But as for me,
I'm free and clear of all these troubles.   400

CREON
Just where and how did you apprehend her?

GUARD
She buried him. That's all you need to know.

CREON
Are you sure you really mean what you say?

GUARD
I saw her myself: she was covering the corpse

that you said we shouldn't. Is that clear enough? 405
CREON
  And how did you catch her in the act?
GUARD
  Here's how it was. When we had gone back,
with your awful threats still fresh in our minds,
we swept all the dust away from the corpse
and fully exposed the moldering body. 410
Then we placed ourselves upwind on the hill,
where we could avoid being hit by the stench.
We roused each other with noisy abuse
whenever someone began to slack off.
This went on until that time of day 415
when the sun had risen high in the sky
and heat poured down. Then all of a sudden
the sky was in turmoil—a huge cyclone
was stirring up dust and filling the plain.
It battered all of the leaves on the trees
and the air was completely choked with it. 420
With eyes shut we weathered the god-sent
    plague.
After a long time it finally died down.
Then there was the girl. She gave a sharp cry,
like the shriek of a bird who suddenly finds
that her bed is empty, her young are gone. 425
In just that way, when she saw the bare corpse,
she started to wail and to call down curses
against the people who had done that thing.
She gathered more of the thirsty dust
and lifting up an elegant urn 430
poured three libations around the corpse.
We rushed right over and arrested her,
which didn't seem to surprise her at all.
We charged her at once with all of the crimes—
both then and now—she didn't deny them, 435
which made me feel both happy and sad.
Escaping troubles makes a man happy,
but to put friends at risk causes him pain.
Still, none of that matters as much to me
as knowing for sure that I will be safe. 440
CREON
  You there, turning your head toward the ground,
do you admit you did it? Or deny it?
ANTIGONE
  Oh, I did it. I would not deny it.

CREON (to the GUARD)
  Go! Take yourself off wherever you want.
  You've been fully cleared from this weighty charge.   445
                                        Exit GUARD.
  But you—yes or no?—were you aware
  there was a proclamation forbidding this?
ANTIGONE
  Yes. How could I not be? It was well known.
CREON
  And yet you dared to ignore this law?
ANTIGONE
  Zeus did not issue that proclamation.   450
  And the Justice of the underworld gods
  did not give laws like that to humans.
  Your proclaiming does not make you so strong
  that you, who are mortal, can override
  the gods' unfailing and unwritten laws.   455
  They're always in force, not just now or then,
  and no one knows when they first appeared.
  I could not have let the gods convict me
  of breaking those laws through fear of some man.
  I knew I would die—how could I not?—   460
  even if you had not proclaimed it.
  If I die early, I count that my gain.
  For someone who has lived with evils
  like mine, how could death not be a gain?
  No, I do not see any cause for grief   465
  in dying this way. Now, if I had left
  my mother's son to lie dead and unburied,
  then I would grieve—but for this, not at all.
  And if you think that what I've done is foolish
  then I'm accused of folly by a fool.   470
CHORUS
  It's clear that her fierce father's untamed heart
  lives on in her. She will not bow to trouble.
CREON
  But you should know that a too-strong will
  is the first to break. It is the toughest iron,
  heated in fire to the greatest hardness,   475
  that is most likely to shatter or crack.
  I have seen high-spirited horses tamed
  by the smallest of bits, and justly so:
  someone's slave has no right to proud thoughts.
  She knew that she was committing an outrage   480
  when she acted against established laws.

And then it was yet another outrage
when she bragged and even laughed about it.
I'm no longer a man—no, she's the man,
if she can do this without paying for it.   485
What if she is my sister's child? She could
be closer than all my most sacred kin;
she would still not escape the worst of deaths—
her sister too. I am convinced that she
was also involved in planning this thing.   490
Bring her out! I just saw her inside
having lost her mind and raving wildly.
A scheming heart is often exposed
while a person's still plotting in the dark.
But I really hate it when someone's caught   495
and tries to put a good face on their crime.
ANTIGONE
Anything you want besides killing me?
CREON
No, nothing! That will give me all I need.
ANTIGONE
Then why wait? Nothing you have said so far
is pleasing to me, and that will not change.   500
And naturally you are not happy with me.
But what more glorious thing could I do
than place my own brother in a grave?
And all these men would say they approved
if fear didn't make them hold their tongues.   505
That's one advantage of being a tyrant:
you can do and say whatever you want.
CREON
You think this way; these other Thebans don't.
ANTIGONE
Oh they do—they just keep their mouths shut.
CREON
Aren't you ashamed to differ from them?   510
ANTIGONE
No shame in honoring my same-mothered brother.
CREON
That wasn't your brother who fought him and died?
ANTIGONE
Yes, my brother from the same mother and father.
CREON
Then why pay a tribute that dishonors him?
ANTIGONE
His dead corpse will not see it that way.   515

CREON
  When you treat him the same as an ungodly traitor . . .
ANTIGONE
  It was his brother, not some slave, who died.
CREON
  Wasting this land, while the other fought for it.
ANTIGONE
  In Hades these rites have the force of law.
CREON
  The good and the bad don't have equal rights.   520
ANTIGONE
  Who knows? They might in the underworld.
CREON
  Even a dead enemy is never a friend.
ANTIGONE
  I like to have friends, not enemies.
CREON
  So go down there and love those friends of yours.
  As long as I live, no woman rules here.   525
          Enter ISMENE.
CHORUS
  I see Ismene at the door,
  looking sad and worried.
  Her face is flushed;
  her cheeks are stained
  with a loving sister's tears.   530
CREON
  You! I didn't see it—that you were a snake,
  hiding in the house to suck my blood.
  I blindly raised two ruinous traitors,
  rebels against my throne. Do you admit
  your part in this crime, or will you play dumb?   535
ISMENE
  Oh yes, I did it—if she agrees, that is.
  I'll take the blame for it along with her.
ANTIGONE
  Justice won't allow that. You didn't want
  to be involved, and I wouldn't let you.
ISMENE
  With you in trouble, I am not ashamed   540
  to be your shipmate on a sea of grief.
ANTIGONE
  The dead know well who really did this thing.
  I don't care for a friend in name alone.

ISMENE
Please don't reject me, sister. Don't keep me
from blessing the dead and dying with you.   545
ANTIGONE
Don't die with me. And don't claim to have done
what you did not. My own death will suffice.
ISMENE
What life is left for me, if I've lost you?
ANTIGONE
Ask Creon! He's the one you look out for.
ISMENE
Why attack me? It gets you nowhere.   550
ANTIGONE
It pains me to mock you—if I'm doing that.
ISMENE
What can I do to help at this point?
ANTIGONE
Save yourself. I don't mind you escaping.
ISMENE
So I should miss out on sharing your death?
ANTIGONE
You made the choice to live, and I to die.   555
ISMENE
True. But I did explain my position.
ANTIGONE
To some your views made sense, to others
       mine.
ISMENE
And in the end we both have equal blame.
ANTIGONE
Take heart, live on! For me my life has been
a kind of death, so I could serve the dead.   560
CREON
One of these girls is turning out to be
an idiot. The other always was.
ISMENE
With all respect, the good sense we are born with
often deserts us when bad times arrive.
CREON
Or when you chose bad acts with bad companions.   565
ISMENE
What kind of life would I want without her?
CREON
Do not speak as if she were still living.

ISMENE
You're going to kill your son's intended bride?
CREON
Oh, there are other fields for him to plow!   *brutha what...*
ISMENE
But these two are so well suited!   570
CREON
I cannot let my sons have evil wives.
ISMENE[3]
Dearest Haemon, your father insults you!
CREON
You get on my nerves with this talk of marriage.
ISMENE
You really will keep her from your own son?
CREON
It's Hades who will prevent the marriage.   575
ISMENE
It seems it's decided that she will die.
CREON
You said it, and I agree. Men, go ahead
and take her inside. And from now on,
these two will stay there as women should.
Yes, even the bold try to run away   580
when Hades looms and the end is in sight.
                    ANTIGONE *and* ISMENE *are led inside.*
CHORUS
Blessed are they who live their lives without
          tasting trouble.
In a house rocked by god-sent turmoil,
disaster spreads through the generations,   585
as when a sea swell
storming from Thrace
charges across the dark depths;
it stirs up black sand
from the bottom,   590
and the wind-battered shore groans when it breaks.

This, I can see, has long been the fate of the
          Labdacid line:[4]

3. The medieval manuscripts on which our Greek text is based assign this line to Ismene,
   but an early printed edition and some commentators assign it to Antigone instead. This
   is an interesting suggestion, and the manuscripts do include many errors and mis-
   attributions, but it would break the typical flow of this kind of line-for-line exchange
   and would make Antigone express feelings for Haemon that she otherwise does not.
4. Labdacus, a grandson of Thebes' founder Cadmus, was the father of Laius and the grandfather of Oedipus. Labdacus died young in battle. Laius abducted and raped his host's son;

Inherited troubles pile onto new ones.   595
The next generation never escapes;
some god knocks them down first.
Now the light that once shielded   600
the last shoots of Oedipus
has been gathered in
by bloody dust of the underworld—
rash words, a Fury[5] in the mind.

O Zeus! What too-bold mortal
could check your power?   605
All-conquering sleep cannot shake it,
or the months' steady progress.
Untouched by time,
you take your stand
on gleaming Olympus.   610
For now, for the future,
as in time past,
this law holds true: no great fortune
without disaster.

To many, wide-ranging hope
is a blessing; others are betrayed   615
by mindless desires:
someone can be oblivious
until they step in the fire.
As a wise man's   620
famous saying goes:
what is bad seems good
to a mind that some god
bends toward disaster.
Disaster strikes all too soon.   625
        Enter HAEMON.
Now here comes Haemon,
your last-born child.
Is he upset
by his fiancée's fate?
Is he mourning his stolen marriage?   630
CREON
    I will find out. There's no call for seercraft.
    Son, now that you have heard the verdict

---

then, after he married Jocasta, they were warned by an oracle that if they had a son, that
son would kill his father, but they did so anyway; when Oedipus was born, they had a
shepherd leave him exposed on a mountainside in the expectation that he would die.
5. The Furies were vengeful underworld goddesses who pursued and tormented wrongdoers.

on your bride-to-be, are you angry at me,
or are you still loyal whatever I do?

HAEMON

I am your son. And you rightly lay out   635
useful precepts for me to follow.
I would not put any marriage ahead
of learning from you when your views are sound.

CREON

Good thinking, my boy. You correctly see
that nothing outweighs your father's advice.   640
That's why a man is eager to breed
obedient offspring for his house:
they will answer his enemies with spite
and honor his friends just as he does.
A man whose children won't cooperate   645
has begotten trouble for himself—
and for his enemies, a chance to gloat.
Son, do not abandon your good sense
for the sake of pleasure with a woman.
It's cold comfort when you wrap your arms   650
around an evil woman who shares your bed.
You hurt yourself when you love someone
        bad.
So spit that girl out: she's our enemy
and can find a husband down in Hades.
I caught her acting in open defiance—   655
her alone out of all of the Thebans.
I will show them now that I wasn't joking:
I'll have her killed. Let her call on Zeus
of kindred blood, but if my family's allowed
to get out of hand, so will everyone else.   660
A man who can manage his household well
is also an upstanding citizen.
I am confident that a man like that
would rule well himself and would gladly be
well ruled by others. He'd stick to his station,   665
a worthy comrade in the storms of war.
But if someone breaks rank and spurns the
        laws
or tries to give orders to the ones in charge,
he won't earn my praise. Whatever leader
the city appoints has to be obeyed   670
in matters big or small, just or unjust.
There's nothing worse than insubordination:
It's this that razes towns and overturns

stable households and drives allies apart.
Most of the people who succeed in life   675
are kept secure by obeying the rules.
Proper order has to be maintained.
No woman should gain the upper hand.
I'd rather fall to a man if I have to:
I can't be seen as weaker than women.   680

CHORUS
Assuming old age has not stolen our wits,
what you are saying makes a lot of sense.

HAEMON
Father, from the gods we get good judgment,
the greatest of all the blessings we have,
I could never claim—and would never want to—   685
that you are not right to say what you do.
But there could be merit in another course.
Where you're concerned, it is my role to see
how people react and whether they fault you.
The thought of your stern face keeps a commoner   690
from saying things you might not want to hear.
But I pick up what is secretly whispered.
The city grieves to see that girl facing
a shameful death that she hardly deserves,
when she performed the most glorious acts: 695
she would not let her own brother be left
lying unburied in the gore where he fell
to be eaten up by birds and wild dogs.
Shouldn't golden honor be her reward?
Thoughts like these are spreading in the dark.   700
Father, for me the surest source of pride
is your success. What greater distinction
can children enjoy than the high renown
of a living father? Or he than theirs?
So don't adopt a narrow point of view—   705
as if only what you say can be correct.
People who assume that they alone
know what to think and how to speak,
and that no one else can have good judgment,
are found to be hollow when you look inside.
For even a clever man, there is no shame   710
in learning more and not being rigid.
You have seen how in winter's stormy streams
the trees that bend can keep their branches safe
while it's the stiffer ones that get uprooted.
And a sailor who has his sheet hauled tight,   715

and gives it no slack, is sure to capsize
and sail along in an upside-down hull.
So let this go and be willing to change.
I may be young, but if I know anything,
I can see that things always go better   720
when a man just naturally knows what's right,
or—since that is so often not the case—
when he can learn from others' good advice.

CHORUS

If he makes a good point, then learn from him,
as he should learn from you; you both spoke well.   725

CREON

So you recommend that men of our age
be taught what to think by someone that young?

HAEMON

Yes, when it's right! I may be young,
but look at my actions and not my years.

CREON

You mean good actions like honoring rebels?   730

HAEMON

I don't say to honor people who do wrong.

CREON

And she's not infected with wrongdoing?

HAEMON

Our fellow Thebans do not think so.

CREON

So the city should tell me how to rule?

HAEMON

Do you hear how young and rash you sound?   735

CREON

How else should I rule but as I see fit?

HAEMON

No city belongs to just one man.

CREON

Isn't the ruler a city's legal owner?

HAEMON

You would be great at running a wasteland.

CREON

Oh, now he's fighting on the woman's side.   740

HAEMON

If you're a woman. It's you I watch out for.

CREON

By charging me with crimes? You worst of sons!

HAEMON

I see you straying beyond what is right.

CREON
    I'm straying when I respect my office?
HAEMON
    There's no respect in trampling gods' honors.   745
CREON
    It's disgusting the way you submit to that woman.
HAEMON
    You won't see me submit to anything shameful.
CREON
    But whatever you say is for that woman.
HAEMON
    And for you, and me, and the gods below.
CREON
    Well, she won't be alive for you to marry.   750
HAEMON
    And when she dies, she will kill someone else.
CREON
    You actually dare to make such threats?
HAEMON
    It's a threat to question empty ideas?
CREON
    You'll regret giving such foolish advice.
HAEMON
    I'd call you a fool, if you weren't my father.   755
CREON
    You woman's slave! Don't give me clever speeches!
HAEMON
    So you want to talk but not to listen?
CREON
    That's what you think? Well, by Mount Olympus,
    you won't get away with this kind of abuse.
    Bring out that hateful thing, so she can die   760
    right now, with her bridegroom looking on.
HAEMON
    Oh no, not me! You are wrong to believe
    that she could die with me nearby. Oh no,
    you will never see my face again:
    rave all you want for people who like it.   765

                                    Exit HAEMON.

CHORUS
    My lord, he's rushed off full of anger.
    A young man in pain has a bitter heart.
CREON
    Let him go and think his superior thoughts!
    He still can't save those two girls from death.

CHORUS
  Do you really intend to kill them both?   770
CREON
  I'll spare the one whose hands are clean. You're right.
CHORUS
  What means of killing do you have in mind?
CREON
  I will take her to a deserted place
  and leave her alive in a rocky cave,
  with just enough food to avoid pollution,   775
  so the city itself will not be tainted.
  She can pray to the only god she reveres—
  Hades—and maybe he'll save her from death.
  Or else she will finally understand
  that revering Hades is a waste of time.   780
CHORUS
  Love, winner of every skirmish!
  Conqueror of our flocks and herds!
  You spend your nights
  on young girls' cheeks.
  You make your way across the sea   785
  and into farmland shelters.
  You are not escaped by deathless gods,
  or mortals who live for a day.
  Knowing you means madness.   790

  You force good people
  onto shameful paths.
  You are the one who has stirred up
  a blood-kin quarrel between these men.
  Desire, which shines in the young bride's eyes,   795
  earns the victory here.
  He takes his seat on a lofty throne
  beside our most honored rules.
  Aphrodite[6] plays to win!   800
        Enter ANTIGONE, *led by* GUARDS.
  I myself forget those rules
  when I see what's happening here.
  I can't hold back my streaming tears
  when Antigone is marching toward
  the place where all must sleep.   805
ANTIGONE
  Citizens of my father's land,

---

6. Olympian goddess of sexual love; her son Eros, or Love, acts on her behalf.

look! Look at me!
I'm heading down my final path,
seeing my final ray of light.
Nothing more is left for me,   810
except that Hades,
who makes all sleep,
leads me alive to Acheron's[7] shore.
No chance for me to be a bride,
no wedding song.   815
I will marry Acheron.

CHORUS
But what about the praise and fame
that follow you to death's dark cave?
You are not struck down by wasting disease.
You are not paying the price of war.   820
You alone of your own free will
descend alive to Hades.

ANTIGONE
I've heard about
our Phrygian guest,[8]
daughter of Tantalus,   825
and her sad, sad death
beside Mount Sipylus.
Encircled by a rocky growth
as if by a clinging vine,
she's worn away by rain and snow
and soaks the ridges with her tears.   830
Put to sleep by destiny,
I am just like her.

CHORUS
She was a goddess, born of a god.
We are merely human beings.   835
It's a great thing for one who dies
if they share honor with the gods,
in their life and after death.

ANTIGONE
You are mocking me!
Can't you wait till I'm gone,   840
you richest men of the city?

7. Acheron was one of the five rivers of the underworld; its name means "river of pain."
8. Niobe came to Thebes to marry King Amphion, to whom she bore many children.
   These were killed by the twin Olympian gods Apollo and Artemis when she claimed to
   have outdone their mother, Leto, who had only borne the two of them. She returned to
   Phrygia as a perpetual mourner and was gradually transformed into a rock that formed
   part of Mount Sipylus. The water that ran down its face was traditionally identified
   with Niobe's tears.

O springs of Dirce!
O Theban ground,
home of splendid chariots!
You I can call as witnesses: 845
how alone I am, with no grieving friends—
what kind of laws are driving me
to a prison burial, a new kind of tomb,
in a horrible state,
neither living nor dead,   850
with no right to settle
either here or there.

CHORUS
Stepping past the limits of daring,
you stumbled, child, on the altar
of justice. Now you pay a penalty   855
passed down from your father.

ANTIGONE
You have touched
on what hurts me most—
constant grief for my poor father
and for all the bitter trials   860
of the famous Labdacid line.
Disaster in a mother's bed,
my parents' incestuous union,
and from the two of them
my own unhappy birth.   865
Now I'll be resettled with them,
unmarried and under a curse.
My brother, your marriage
was disastrous too.[9] Your death   870
destroys me while I still live.

CHORUS
There's something holy in your devotion,
yet for the one who holds the power,
no overstepping can be allowed.
Your willful temper has destroyed you.   875

ANTIGONE
No mourners, no friends,
no wedding! In misery
I am led down the road ahead.
I no longer am allowed
to see the sacred light.   880

---

9. Polyneices secured his alliance with the Argives by marrying Argeia, daughter of King
   Adrastus.

Yet there are no sad cries,
no tears shed for my fate.

CREON

Look, no one who's dying would ever stop
singing laments if they did any good.
Won't you take her off and shut her away,   885
confined in a tomb, like I told you to?
I want you to leave her completely alone.
She can die if she likes or live on there,
and we'll be guilt-free where she's concerned.
But she has lost the right to settle here above.   890

ANTIGONE

My tomb, my wedding place, that deep-dug
        cave,
that tightly guarded room, through which I go
to join my own. Of them, Persephone[1]
has already gathered in so many—
I the latest and by far the saddest one,   895
not having had my proper share of life.
Still, I can enter there with confidence
that I am loved and welcomed by my father,
by you as well, my mother, and by you,
my dearest brother: when you had died,   900
I washed your body with my own two hands
and poured libations at your tomb. And now,
for all that care, I get this reward.
The wise can see I'm right to put you first.
If it were my children or a dead husband   905
who lay there rotting, then I would not
have defied the city to take on this service.
And what's the law that underlies this claim?
If a husband dies, I can get another,
or have a new man's child if the first one's die.   910
But both my parents are now in Hades:
I have no way to get a new brother.
Because of that law, I honor you more.
In Creon's view, I've done something wrong,
an act of daring that fills him with dread.   915
So he's having me seized and led away
with no chance of marriage, no wedding song,
no chance of being a wife or a mother.
Alone, in despair, deserted by friends,
I go, still alive, to the caves of the dead.   920

(handwritten margin note:) ? Why for her brother you + not for her their children + husband

1. Wife of Hades; queen of the underworld.

What have I done to offend the gods?
Why should I even look to the gods?
Who can I call on? I honored the gods
and for that I'm convicted of sacrilege.
If the gods truly think that this is right,   925
what I suffer will teach me that I am wrong.
But if these men are wrong, then they should
    suffer
evils that match their mistreatment of me.

CHORUS
Still the same windy gusts,
storms of the soul, possess her.   930

CREON
And these men will pay with their tears
because they still haven't led her away.

ANTIGONE
Oh! Those words mean death
is very near.

CREON
I'm not offering any hope: 935
the prior sentence stands.

ANTIGONE
O Thebes, my father's city!
O gods of our family line!
The time has come. They are taking me now.
Look at me, you leaders of Thebes,   940
the last living member of your royal house.
See who is making me suffer like this,
for honoring what is sacred.

Exit ANTIGONE, led by GUARDS.

CHORUS[2]
Danaë too had to trade
heavenly daylight   945
for a bronze-bound house.
She was locked up,
entombed in her room,
and yet she came—o child!—from a noble line

---

2. The Chorus responds to Antigone's departure to be locked up in a cave by evoking three mythological figures who had some association with caves or confinement and whose stories illustrate the inescapability of fate (though other connections may also be suggested). Danaë was shut up in a tower by her father because of a prophecy that her son would kill him, but she was impregnated by Zeus in the form of golden rain and bore the hero Perseus. Lycurgus was one of several arrogant rulers punished for denying the divinity of Dionysus. The final and most obscure example is Boreas' daughter Cleopatra; after she was divorced by Phineus (and possibly imprisoned), his second wife attacked their sons.

and raised a son from Zeus' golden stream. 950
The power of fate is uncanny.
Nothing can escape it—not wealth,
not walls, not strength in war,
not pitch-dark ships that race across the sea.

And Dryas' son Lycurgus, 955
the hot-tempered Edonian king,
was also confined to a rocky cell,
for raging at Dionysus.
His swelling madness drained away,
and he could see that he'd been mad, 960
to strike at a god with taunting words.
When he tried to put a stop
to the maenads' Bacchic[3] cries
and their sacred torches,
he incited their shrill-piping Muse. 965

In Thrace, where the Bosporus[4] joins
one dark sea to another,
there lies a city, Salmydessos. 970
Ares lives near, and he could see
the savage blinding of Phineus' sons.
Phineus' wife scratched out their eyes,
empty circles demanding revenge,
assaulted by her bloody hands 975
and the sharp point of her shuttle.

Wasting away, they wept for their wounds
and their mother's unhappy marriage. 980
Yet she came from a noble line,
the ancient house of Erechtheus.
She was raised in distant caves,
among her father's gusting winds,
daughter of Boreas,[5] swift as a horse. 985
But even she was caught—o child!—
by the ever-lasting Fates.[6]
    Enter TEIRESIAS, *led by a boy.*

3. Adjective derived from Bacchus, another name for Dionysus. Maenads were female followers of Dionysus, who worshiped him in a state of ecstatic possession.
4. Strait in present-day Turkey that joins the Sea of Marmara (and through it the Aegean Sea) to the Black Sea; border between Europe, specifically the region known as Thrace, and Asia.
5. God of the north wind.
6. The Fates, or Moirai, were three powerful goddesses who determined each individual's destiny at birth.

TEIRESIAS
  Elders of Thebes, the two of us have come
  along a road that only one has seen;
  the blind need a guide to show them the way.   990
CREON
  Honored Teiresias, what is the matter?
TEIRESIAS
  I'll tell you. Pay attention—I'm a prophet.
CREON
  I have never rejected your advice before.
TEIRESIAS
  That is how you've kept this city on course.
CREON
  I can certainly affirm that it's been a help.   995
TEIRESIAS
  You should know you're on the razor's edge again.
CREON
  How so? You make me shudder with those words.
TEIRESIAS
  The signs that I know how to read will tell you.
  When I came to the seat of divination,
  the ancient refuge for birds of all kinds,   1000
  I heard them making unfamiliar sounds,
  frenzied shrieks and angry chitter-chatter,
  and I could tell from their whirring wings
  that they tore at each other with bloody claws.
  In fright, I started making sacrifices,   1005
  and tried to light a flame upon the altar,
  but Hephaestus'[7] fire would not flare up.
  A slimy liquid dripped off the thigh bones,
  smoking and spitting on the smoldering ashes,
  and drops of bile were spread throughout the air.   1010
  The fat that covered those thigh bones slid off.
  This boy explained that my seercraft had failed,
  that my prophetic rites signified nothing.
  For he guides me while I guide others.
  Your stubborn views have made the city sick,   1015
  Our altars and our household fires are piled
  with human flesh that greedy birds and dogs
  bring back as food from Oedipus' fallen son.
  When we sacrifice, the gods will not accept
  the prayers we offer or the bones we burn.   1020
  The shrieking birds no longer give us signs,

---

7. Olympian god, blacksmith associated with fire and metalworking.

now that they've tasted human fat and blood.
So you must put your mind to this, my friend.
Mistakes are made by every human being.
The man who, when he stumbles into trouble,   1025
gets straight to work and tries to heal the damage
can overcome his folly and misfortune.
It's stubbornness that marks you out as stupid.
Let the dead be. Stop kicking a corpse.
What is so brave about killing a dead man?   1030
I wish you well and my advice is good.
It's a fine thing to profit from good advice.

CREON
Old man! I'm just a target for you all,
and I've been hit by your prophetic art.
For a long time, the members of your tribe   1035
have been busily buying and selling me.
Go on with your trading and profiteering.
Import all the Persian electrum you want
and Indian gold.[8] You will not get me
to cover that corpse. Why, if Zeus' eagles   1040
snatch up his flesh and fly to Zeus' throne,
I won't start fretting about pollution
and agree to the burial because of that.
We have no power to pollute the gods.
But, old Teiresias, the cleverest men   1045
come to grief when they sweetly say
things that are shameful, for the sake of gain.

TEIRESIAS
No!
Doesn't anyone know or understand . . .

CREON
Know what? What weighty point are you making?

TEIRESIAS
That nothing's better than having good judgment.   1050

CREON
And nothing is worse than stupidity.

TEIRESIAS
And yet you are riddled with that disease.

CREON
I won't be rude responding to a prophet.

8. Riches associated with the wealthy Persian Empire. The Greeks believed that much of
the wealth of the empire came from gold imported from India. Electrum is a naturally
occurring alloy of silver and gold that was mined near Sardis, an important ancient city
in present-day western Turkey.

TEIRESIAS
You're rude when you call my prophecies false.
CREON
They are, because all prophets worship money.　　　1055
TEIRESIAS
And all tyrants adore illegal payments.
CREON
You know you're denouncing a high-placed ruler?
TEIRESIAS
I helped you save this city that you now rule.
CREON
You have prophetic skill, but you're dishonest.
TEIRESIAS
You'll make me say what's better left unsaid.　　　1060
CREON
Oh, bring it all up, but just not for gain.
TEIRESIAS
Do you really believe that that's my motive?
CREON
Don't think that you can barter my beliefs.
TEIRESIAS
Then don't expect that you will see the sun
make many circuits of its daily track　　　1065
before you have to answer for those corpses
with one that comes from your own body:
you deport a living person to a tomb,
sending someone to Hades who should stay here,
and keep someone here who belongs down there,　　　1070
a dispossessed and defiled dead body.
And so, you have brutally interfered
where you and the upper gods have no place,
and vicious Furies are lying in wait,
divine avengers who will see that you　　　1075
are also entangled in evils like these.
See if you really think I've been bribed.
It won't be long before your house is filled
with wailing cries of men and women.
The other cities have all turned on you,　　　1080
since body parts are being laid to rest
in dogs, wild beasts, and soaring birds, who bear
a sordid stench to their communal hearths.
You have made me angry, so I have aimed
my sturdy arrows straight at your heart,　　　1085
and you will not outrun their fiery sting.

Now you should take me home again, my boy.
This man can vent his rage on younger men,
and maybe he will learn to cultivate
a kinder tongue and better frame of mind.   1090

Exit TEIRESIAS.

CHORUS
Creon, what that man said before he left
was terrifying. And in all the years
since my hair went gray, he has never been known
to tell us anything that was not true.

CREON
I know that, and it worries me. I dread   1095
the thought of yielding, but to hold my ground
and drive myself to ruin would be dreadful too.

CHORUS
Son of Menoeceus, take some good advice.

CREON
Just tell me! I'll do whatever you suggest.

CHORUS
Free that girl from her underground prison   1100
and make a tomb for the cast-off body.

CREON
So you would advise me to just give in?

CHORUS
And right away! For the swift-footed Furies
can easily outpace slow-witted mortals.

CREON
I don't want to give in. But there's no point   1105
in fighting back. I will do what I have to.

CHORUS
So go! So do it! Don't leave it to others.

CREON
I will go right now. And I order these men
to get the others and pick up some axes,
then head to that place you can see over there.   1110
My mind has been changed, and therefore I,
the one who confined her, will set her free.
It now seems horribly clear that it's best
always to follow well-established laws.

Exit CREON, *with his attendants.*

CHORUS
God called by many names,

delight of Cadmus' daughter,[9]
glorious child of thundering Zeus!
In famous Italy[1] you are known,
and in the valleys of Eleusis,
where Demeter[2] welcomes all,
and here in Thebes, o Bacchic god!,
home of the bacchante women,
here by the river Ismenus,
where the dragon's teeth were sown.[3] 1117

1125

You appear on the rocky peaks
of Delphi's[4] double mountain,
lit by the flames of smoky torches,
where Corycian maenads dance
by the fountain of Castalia. 1130
From Nysa's ivy-covered hill,
and the vineyards of the coast,
you are sent to the streets of Thebes,
where you hear immortal voices 1135
shouting out your joyous cry.

To Thebes, held in highest honor
by you and by your stricken mother,
the victim of the lightning bolt,
this city gripped by wracking plague, 1140
come and bring your healing presence!
Make your way along Parnassus;
travel across the echoing strait! 1145

You, who are the chorus leader
of the fire-breathing stars,
master of nocturnal voices,
child of Zeus, appear to us!,

9. Dionysus was the son of Zeus and Semele, the daughter of Cadmus, the founder of Thebes. Semele was killed when she asked Zeus to come to her in his true form and he appeared as a thunderbolt. She was pregnant with Dionysus, whom Zeus saved and had raised by nymphs in a mountainous region called Nysa, traditionally identified with several different locations.
1. By the fifth century B.C.E., there were numerous Greek colonies in southern Italy.
2. Olympian goddess of agriculture and mystical rebirth, with an important cult center near Athens, in Eleusis.
3. The first inhabitants of Thebes came from the earth; after killing a dragon, Cadmus sowed its teeth in the ground like seeds, and men grew up from them.
4. A cult center, location of a major oracle of the prophetic god Apollo but also a site of Dionysian worship; its landmarks include a spring, Castalia, and a mountain with two peaks, Parnassus, which contained the cave known as Corycia.

followed by your frenzied Thyiads[5]   1150
who sing and dance throughout the night
to honor lord Iacchus.
   Enter the MESSENGER.

MESSENGER
 O you who live in Cadmus' ancient city,   1155
 I'd never want to judge a person's life
 as good or bad, whatever their condition,
 since luck keeps casting down and raising up
 the ones who prosper and the ones who don't.
 We can't predict that things will stay the same.   1160
 For Creon once was someone that I envied:
 he saved our land when enemies attacked us;
 he had assumed a king's prerogatives
 and guided us; and he had thriving sons.
 Now all of that is gone. And when life's joys   1165
 desert a man, I can't consider him
 a living person—he's just a breathing corpse.
 Sure, you can have a house that's crammed with
  wealth
 and live the way a tyrant does. But if
 you can't enjoy the things you own, well then,   1170
 I would not give a wisp of smoke for them.
CHORUS
 What's your sad news about the royal family?
MESSENGER
 They're dead! And those still living are to blame.
CHORUS
 Tell me! Who is the killer? Who lies dead?
MESSENGER
 Haemon is dead: he brought it on himself.   1175
CHORUS
 By his father's hand or by his own?
MESSENGER
 His own, in anger at his murderous father.
CHORUS
 O prophet! It seems that what you said was true!
MESSENGER
 So now it's time to plan for what comes next.
   Enter EURYDICE.
CHORUS
 And Creon's sad-faced wife Eurydice   1180

5. Local nymphs (female nature divinities) of Delphi, who worship Dionysus under one of
 his cult names, Iacchus.

is here. Did she just leave her house by chance,
or has she heard the news about her son?

EURYDICE

O Thebans gathered here, I heard the news
as I was coming out the door. I planned
to go and pray to the goddess Athena.[6]   1185
I was pulling back the bolt that holds the gate
when word of our family's troubles hit me.
I was terrified, and I tumbled back
and into the arms of my household slaves.
Repeat the story once again for me.   1190
I am used to hearing about disasters.

MESSENGER

My honored queen, I was there myself,
and I will give you an exact account.
Why should I tell a softer version now,
and later be exposed as a liar?   1195
It is always better to tell the truth.
I went with your husband to that plain,
where Polyneices' dog-chewed corpse still lay.
There, praying to Pluto and to Hecate,[7]
goddess of crossroads, to hold back their anger,   1200
we washed the body with sacred water,
then gathered branches and burned the remains.
We built a tall mound out of Theban earth,
and left at once for the stony cave,
the poor girl's deadly bridal chamber.   1205
From far away we heard sounds of wailing
coming from that unholy bedroom;
someone ran back to tell our master Creon.
As he got closer, he was assailed
by bitter shouts that were hard to make out.   1210
He moaned: "I'm like a heartsick prophet,
and can foresee that I have started down
the hardest road that I will ever take.
That voice is my son's. So now, you men,
go at once to the tomb and enter through   1215
the jagged hole that has been opened up,
and let me know if that is Haemon's voice
or if I'm being hoodwinked by the gods."
In keeping with our wretched master's orders

---

6. Olympian goddess, patron of Athens, associated with intelligence, just wars, and
women's crafts, especially weaving.
7. A minor goddess associated with witchcraft, magic, and the passage to the underworld.
Pluto: another name for Hades.

we approached the cave and looked inside: 1220
we saw her hanging, her neck in a noose
that was made from a twisted piece of cloth;
he was there too with his arms around her,
lamenting the bride he had lost to death,
his ruined marriage, and his father's crimes.   1225
When Creon saw this, he groaned and went in,
and as he bore down on his son he cried out:
"You poor fool! How could you be so rash?
Has all this trouble made you lose your mind?
I beg, I pray, will you please come here."   1230
His son just looked at him with wild-beast eyes;
he gave no answer but spat on his father
and drew his sword. But Creon fell back,
so Haemon missed. In disgust with himself,
he bent over the sword and swiftly drove   1235
half its length into his ribs. And still alive,
he clasped the woman in his shaking arm,
and as he gasped for breath, he spurted out
a stream of bloody drops on her white cheek.
And there he lies, a corpse beside a corpse.   1240
That poor boy was married in the house
of Death. His story clearly proves the point:
there is nothing worse than faulty judgment.

                                        Exit EURYDICE.

CHORUS
   Now what about this? The queen is gone.
   She simply left without saying a word.   1245

MESSENGER
   I'm worried too, but I hope that it means
   that now that she's learned of her son's sad end
   she does not want a citywide lament,
   and will ask her household to grieve in private.
   She has the wisdom to avoid missteps.   1250

CHORUS
   I cannot say. But I'm just as alarmed
   by total silence as by pointless shouting.

MESSENGER
   Then I will go inside so I can see
   if she's been hiding some secret plan
   deep inside her troubled heart. You are right: 1255
   total silence is alarming.

                                        Exit MESSENGER.

        Enter CREON.

CHORUS

    Now here's the king, and in his arms
    he bears a clear memorial to his ruin.
    If I can speak my mind, I have to say
    this is the result of his own mistakes.   1260

CREON

    Oh!
    Oh, how I've blundered,
    with my ruinous will!
    Look! Killers and victims
    from the same clan,
    all because of my stupid ideas.   1265
    My son—hardly grown and now dead!
    It was my folly,
    mine, not yours,
    that made you leave so young.

CHORUS

    How hard—that you should see what's right too late.   1270

CREON

    So hard!
    I've learned that now, to my great sorrow.
    But then, a god struck at my head
    and pushed me into vicious paths
    so all my joy was trampled down.   1275
    Human troubles are hard to bear.

        Enter MESSENGER.

MESSENGER

    My lord, you own one burden of sorrow,
    which you now carry in your arms. Inside,
    you'll find another stored up in the house.   1280

CREON

    What greater sorrow could follow these?

MESSENGER

    Your wife has died of blows she dealt herself,
    keeping a mother's faith with this poor corpse.

CREON

    Why?
    Foul harbor of Hades,
    why must you destroy me?
    And you, with your bad news,   1285
    what are you saying?
    You kill me all over again
    with your terrible tale:
    bloody slaughter,   1290

a woman's death,
on top of this disaster.
          Enter attendants, carrying EURYDICE's *body.*
MESSENGER
    See for yourself. They are bringing her out.
CREON
    Oh!
    I'm looking at a second disaster!   1295
    What more, what more is to come?
    Here I am holding my own son's corpse.
    And now I see this other body.
    Poor mother! Poor child!   1300
MESSENGER
    There by the altar, with a sharpened knife
                              . . .[8]
    she let her eyes go dark, with loud laments
    for the empty bed of dead Megareus,[9]
    and now for this son too. And she called down
    on you, your own child's killer, bitter curses.   1305
CREON
    Oh, oh, oh!
    That fills me with dread!
    Can someone find a sword
    and plunge its double blade into my heart?
    I am undone, I'm broken down   1310
    by evil after evil!
MESSENGER
    Yes! As she died, this woman here
    declared you guilty of both of those deaths.
CREON
    So tell me. How exactly was she killed?
MESSENGER
    As soon as she learned what her son had suffered,   1315
    she took up a knife and stabbed her own heart.
CREON
    Oh no! The blame for this
    will never pass to someone else!
    I am the one, I am the killer,
    I admit it: that is the truth.   1320
    You men, just take me, take me away!
    All I am is nothing.   1325

8. A line is evidently missing here from our manuscripts.
9. The other son of Creon and Eurydice, who was sacrificed to secure the Theban victory over the Argives.

CHORUS
A good thought under the circumstances:
in times of trouble, the quicker the better.

CREON
Let it come! Let it come,
most welcome death,
and the end of my days.   1330
Let it come! Let it come!
I cannot face another day.

CHORUS
That is for the future, but right now
we have to attend to matters at hand.   1335

CREON
But all I long for is summed up in that prayer.

CHORUS
Don't think about praying. For mortals like us.
there is no escaping our bad fortunes.

CREON
Just get my worthless self away from here.
I killed you, my son, without meaning to.   1340
And o my poor wife! I killed you too.
I have no one to lean on for support.
Nothing I've done turned out as I planned.   1345
I am beaten down, crushed by disaster.

CHORUS
For a good life, what's needed most
is sound understanding
and never to cross the gods.   1350
The blows that punish haughty boasts
teach us wisdom
as we grow old.

CONTEXTS

Ancient Contexts

LYSIAS

The Athenians of the classical period (the fifth and fourth centuries B.C.E.) conducted an annual public funeral for those who had died in combat during the previous year. This included a speech delivered by a leading citizen that not only praised the dead for their courage and self-sacrifice but also celebrated Athens as a city worth dying for. Our surviving record includes several literary representations of such speeches, which give a good sense of the main themes of Athenian patriotic rhetoric. One is a famous version of the speech given by the prominent politician Pericles in 431 B.C.E., after the first year of the Peloponnesian War, reconstructed by the historian Thucydides. Among the forms of excellence that make Athens stand out from other cities, Pericles includes the respect for unwritten laws that Antigone champions in her confrontation with Creon: "We are tolerant of each other where private matters are concerned, but we are especially law-abiding in our public life, motivated by caution in our obedience to whoever is in power and to the laws, especially those established to help the mistreated and those that are unwritten but which, when broken, call forth unanimous shame" (Thucydides 2.37). Another is by the fourth-century speech-writer Lysias. This was ostensibly composed for delivery in 395, but it could not have been delivered by Lysias himself, since he was not an Athenian citizen. It may have been written for someone else to deliver or simply as a literary exercise. In any case, it presents the more conventional account of the burial of the Seven against Thebes, an event in which the Athenians took great pride but from which Sophocles departed in devising the plot of *Antigone*.

Funeral Oration[†]

When Adrastus [Polyneices' Argive ally] and Polyneices had waged war on Thebes and had been defeated in battle, the Thebans would not allow them to bury the bodies of the dead. The Athenians took the position that those men, if they acted wrongly, had paid the fullest possible penalty by dying; meanwhile the gods below were not

† From *Lysias* 2.7–10. Translated by the editor of this Norton Critical Edition.

45

receiving what was owed to them and the gods above were being
treated impiously because sacred places were being polluted. First
they sent heralds and asked permission to take up the bodies, thinking that brave men should punish their enemies while they were
alive, but that to make a show of courage against the bodies of the
dead was a sign of insecurity. When they could not get what they
asked for, they went to war against them, even though there was no
previous quarrel between themselves and the Thebans. They did not
do this to please the Argives who were still alive, but because they
considered that those who had died deserved the customary rites.
So they put themselves in danger for the sake of both sides: for the
Thebans so that they would no longer offend the gods by mistreating
the dead; for the Argives so that they would not return home without their ancestral honor, deprived of the proper rites of the Greeks,
and cut off from the hope of burial that all people share.

That was their reasoning and, accepting that all men face the
same fortunes in war, they took on many enemies but, because they
had justice as their ally, they defeated them in combat. They did not
become so buoyed up by success that they sought any further punishment for the Thebans, but simply displayed their own virtue in
response to the Thebans' impiety. They collected the prize they had
come for—the bodies of the Argives—and they buried them in their
own territory, at Eleusis. That was how they acted in their treatment
of the Seven against Thebes who had died.

HERODOTUS

This passage from *The Histories* of Herodotus, the first full-scale work
of narrative history in the western tradition, is widely thought to be the
source for Antigone's reasoning at lines 908–13, where she makes the
challenging claim that she would not have done for a husband or son
what she did for her brother Polyneices. The argument better fits the
circumstances of the woman in this story, who has to make a choice
among actual relatives, than those of Antigone, who is speaking hypo-
thetically; there is some evidence that Sophocles and Herodotus were
friends as well as contemporaries; and there are several passages in
other plays of Sophocles that appear to have been influenced by *The
Histories*. In this episode, the Persian king Darius comes to suspect that
his former confederate Intaphernes is planning a revolt against him.

From The Histories[†]

Believing that Intaphernes and his relatives were plotting to over-
throw him, Darius had Intaphernes himself and his sons and all his

† From *The Histories* 3.119.3–7. Translated by the editor of this Norton Critical Edition.

male relatives bound and condemned to death. Intaphernes' wife kept going to the palace doors and weeping and wailing. She did this over and over again, until Darius felt sorry for her and sent her a messenger, who told her, "Lady, King Darius will spare the life of one of your condemned relatives, whichever of them you choose." She gave the matter some thought, and responded, "If the King will grant me the life of just one of them, I choose my brother." When Darius heard this, he was amazed and sent the messenger back to her for an explanation: "Lady, the King asks what is your reason for putting aside your husband and your children and choosing your brother, who is less closely related to you than your children and less beloved than your husband." She replied, "O King, god willing I could have another husband, and other children if I lose these ones. But my father and mother are no longer alive, so there is no way I could have another brother. That is the reasoning behind what I said." Darius admired her good sense and showed his favor by sending back to her both the one she had asked for and her oldest son. Then he had all the rest put to death.

Modern Responses

VIRGINIA WOOLF

The English novelist, essayist, and cultural critic Virginia Woolf (1882–1941) was drawn to the heroines of Greek tragedy, especially Antigone and Electra as Sophocles portrayed her, for their moral clarity, emotional directness, and piercing voices. In *Three Guineas* (1938), a book-length exposition of her pacificist and feminist ideas, Woolf identifies Antigone as a model for principled, outspoken women of her own day. But she also points to the ways in which, as a fully imagined drama, Sophocles' *Antigone* resists reduction to propaganda—as do the most successful of its many reworkings.

From Three Guineas[†]

* * * It is impossible to judge any book from a translation, yet even when thus read the *Antigone* is clearly one of the great masterpieces of dramatic literature. Nevertheless, it could undoubtedly be made, if necessary, into anti-Fascist propaganda. Antigone herself could be transformed either into Mrs. Pankhurst, who broke a window and was imprisoned in Holloway; or into Frau Pommer, the wife of a Prussian mines official at Essen, who said: "'The thorn of hatred has been driven deep enough into the people by the religious conflicts, and it is high time that the men of today disappeared.' . . . She has been arrested and is to be tried on a charge of insulting and slandering the State and the Nazi movement." (*The Times*, August 12th, 1935.) Antigone's crime was of much the same nature and was punished in much the same way. Her words, "See what I suffer, and from whom, because I feared to cast away the fear of heaven! . . . And what law of heaven have I transgressed? Why, hapless one, should I look to the gods any more—what ally should I

† From *Three Guineas: Annotated and with an Introduction* by Jane Marcus, ed. Mark Hussey (New York: Houghton Mifflin Harcourt, 2006), pp. 201–02. Copyright © 1938 by Harcourt Inc. Copyright renewed 1966 by Leonard Woolf. Used by permission of HarperCollins Publisher and the Society of Authors as the Literary Representative of the Estate of Virginia Woolf.

invoke—when by piety I have earned the name of impious?" could
be spoken either by Mrs. Pankhurst, or by Frau Pommer; and are
certainly topical. Creon, again, who "thrust the children of the sun-
light to the shades, and ruthlessly lodged a living soul in the grave";
who held that "disobedience is the worst of evils," and that "whom-
soever the city may appoint, that man must be obeyed, in little
things and great, in just things and unjust" is typical of certain
politicians in the past, and of Herr Hitler and Signor Mussolini in
the present. But though it is easy to squeeze these characters into
up-to-date dress, it is impossible to keep them there. They suggest
too much; when the curtain falls we sympathize, it may be noted,
even with Creon himself. This result, to the propagandist undesir-
able, would seem to be due to the fact that Sophocles (even in a
translation) uses freely all the faculties that can be possessed by a
writer; and suggests, therefore, that if we use art to propagate
political opinions, we must force the artist to clip and cabin his
gift to do us a cheap and passing service. Literature will suffer the
same mutilation that the mule has suffered; and there will be no
more horses.

ATHOL FUGARD, JOHN KANI, AND
WINSTON NTSHONA

In this 1973 play, set in apartheid-era South Africa, two men imprisoned on Robben Island (where Nelson Mandela was held from 1964 to
1982) present a version of *Antigone* as their contribution to a concert
put on by inmates. John, who plays Creon, is also the director. Winston, who plays Antigone, has had to overcome his resistance to portraying a woman (though it is worth nothing that in the different
cultural setting of classical Athens, men playing women was the norm):
"you think I don't know what will happen after that? . . . Every time I
run to the quarry . . . 'Nyah . . . nyah . . . Here comes Antigone! . . .
Help the poor lady!' . . . I didn't walk with those men and burn my
bloody passbook in front of that police station, and have a magistrate
send me here for life so that he can dress me up like a woman and
make a bloody fool of me." Shortly before the performance, the men
learn that John, but not Winston, will soon be released.

   See Betine van Zyl Smit's essay in the Criticism section of this volume for a fuller discussion of the play's historical context.

From The Island[†]

Scene Four

The two men convert their cell-area into a stage for the prison concert. Their blankets are hung to provide a makeshift back-drop behind which Winston disappears with their props. John comes forward and addresses the audience. He is not yet in his Creon costume.

JOHN. Captain Prinsloo, Hodoshe,[1] Warders, . . . and Gentlemen! Two brothers of the House of Labdacus found themselves on opposite sides in battle, the one defending the State, the other attacking it. They both died on the battlefield. King Creon, Head of the State, decided that the one who had defended the State would be buried with all religious rites due to the noble dead. But the other one, the traitor Polynices, who had come back from exile intending to burn and destroy his fatherland, to drink the blood of his masters, was to have no grave, no mourning. He was to lie on the open fields to rot, or at most be food for the jackals. It was a law. But Antigone, their sister, defied the law and buried the body of her brother Polynices. She was caught and arrested. That is why tonight the Hodoshe Span, Cell Forty-two, presents for your entertainment: 'The Trial and Punishment of Antigone'.

[*He disappears behind the blankets. They simulate a fanfare of trumpets. At its height the blankets open and he steps out as Creon. In addition to his pendant, there is some sort of crown and a blanket draped over his shoulders as a robe.*]

My People! Creon stands before his palace and greets you! Stop! Stop! What's that I hear? You, good man, speak up. Did I hear 'Hail the King'? My good people, I am your *servant* . . . a happy one, but still your servant. How many times must I ask you, implore you to see in these symbols of office nothing more, or less, than you would in the uniform of the humblest menial in your house. Creon's crown is as simple, and I hope as clean, as the apron Nanny wears. And even as Nanny smiles and is your happy servant because she sees her charge . . . your child! . . . waxing fat in that little cradle, so too does Creon—your obedient servant!—stand here and smile. For what does he see? Fatness

---

† From *Sizwe Bansi Is Dead* and *The Island* (New York: Viking Press, 1976), pp. 73–77. Reprinted with permission. Note is by the editor of this Norton Critical Edition.
1. The Xhosa word for a kind of fly that lays its eggs in dead bodies; here the nickname of a particularly hated prison guard.

and happiness! How else does one measure the success of a state?
By the sumptuousness of the palaces built for its king and
princes? The magnificence of the temples erected to its gods?
The achievements of its scientists and technicians who can now
send rockets to the moon? No! These count for nothing beside
the fatness and happiness of its people.

But have you ever paused to ask yourself whose responsibility
it is to maintain that fatness and happiness? The answer is
simple, is it not? . . . your servant the king! But have you then
gone on to ask yourself what does the king need to maintain this
happy state of affairs? What, other than his silly crown, are the
tools with which a king fashions the happiness of his people? The
answer is equally simple, my good people. The law! Yes. The law.
A three-lettered word, and how many times haven't you glibly
used it, never bothering to ask yourselves, 'What then is the law?'
Or if you have, then making recourse to such clichés as 'the law
states this . . . or the law states that'. The law states or maintains
nothing, good people. The law defends! The law is no more or
less than a shield in your faithful servant's hand to protect YOU!
But even as a shield would be useless in one hand, to defend,
without a sword in the other, to strike . . . so too the law has its
edge. The penalty! We have come through difficult times. I am
sure it is needless for me to remind you of the constant troubles
on our borders . . . those despicable rats who would gnaw away at
our fatness and happiness. We have been diligent in dealing with
them. But unfortunately there are still at large subversive elements . . . there are still amongst us a few rats that are not satis-
fied and to them I must show this face of Creon . . . so different
to the one that hails my happy people! It is with a heavy heart,
and you shall see why soon enough, that I must tell you that we
have caught another one. That is why I have assembled you here.
Let what follows be a living lesson for those among you misguided enough still to harbour sympathy for rats! The shield has
defended. Now the sword must strike!

Bring in the accused.

[*Winston, dressed as Antigone, enters. He wears the wig, the
necklace of nails, and a blanket around his waist as a skirt.*]

Your name!

WINSTON.   Antigone, daughter of Oedipus, sister of Eteocles and
Polynices.

JOHN.   You are accused that, in defiance of the law, you buried the
body of the traitor Polynices.

WINSTON.   I buried the body of my brother Polynices.

JOHN.   Did you know there was a law forbidding that?

WINSTON.   Yes.

JOHN.   Yet you defied it.

WINSTON.   Yes.

JOHN.   Did you know the consequences of such defiance?

WINSTON.   Yes.

JOHN.   What did you plead to the charges laid against you? Guilty or Not Guilty?

WINSTON.   Guilty.

JOHN.   Antigone, you have pleaded guilty. Is there anything you wish to say in mitigation? This is your last chance. Speak.

WINSTON.   Who made the law forbidding the burial of my brother?

JOHN.   The State.

WINSTON.   Who is the State?

JOHN.   As King I am its manifest symbol.

WINSTON.   So you made the law.

JOHN.   Yes, for the State.

WINSTON.   Are you God?

JOHN.   Watch your words, little girl!

WINSTON.   You said it was my chance to speak.

JOHN.   But not to ridicule.

WINSTON.   I've got no time to waste on that. Your sentence on my life hangs waiting on your lips.

JOHN.   Then speak on.

WINSTON.   When Polynices died in battle, all that remained was the empty husk of his body. He could neither harm nor help any man again. What lay on the battlefield waiting for Hodoshe to turn rotten, belonged to God. You are only a man, Creon. Even as there are laws made by men, so too there are others that come from God. He watches my soul for a transgression even as your spies hide in the bush at night to see who is transgressing your laws. Guilty against God I will not be for any man on this earth. Even without your law, Creon, and the threat of death to whoever defied it, I know I must die. Because of your law and my defiance, that fate is now very near. So much the better. Your threat is nothing to me, Creon. But if I had let my mother's son, a Son of the Land, lie there as food for the carrion fly, Hodoshe, my soul would never have known peace. Do you understand anything of what I am saying, Creon?

JOHN.   Your words reveal only that obstinacy of spirit which has brought nothing but tragedy to your people. First you break the law. Now you insult the State.

WINSTON.   Just because I ask you to remember that you are only a man?

JOHN.   And to add insult to injury you gloat over your deeds! No, Antigone, you will not escape with impunity. Were you my own child you would not escape full punishment.

WINSTON.   Full punishment? Would you like to do more than just kill me?

JOHN.   That is all I wish.

WINSTON.   Then let us not waste any time. Stop talking. I buried my brother. That is an honourable thing, Creon. All these people in your state would say so too, if fear of you and another law did not force them into silence.

JOHN.   You are wrong. None of my people think the way you do.

WINSTON.   Yes they do, but no one dares tell you so. You will not sleep peacefully, Creon.

JOHN.   You add shamelessness to your crimes, Antigone.

WINSTON.   I do not feel any shame at having honoured my brother.

JOHN.   Was he that died with him not also your brother?

WINSTON.   He was.

JOHN.   And so you honour the one and insult the other.

WINSTON.   I shared my love, not my hate.

JOHN.   Go then and share your love among the dead. I will have no rats' law here while yet I live.

WINSTON.   We are wasting time, Creon. Stop talking. Your words defeat your purpose. They are prolonging my life.

JOHN [*again addressing the audience*].   You have heard all the relevant facts. Needless now to call the state witnesses who would testify beyond reasonable doubt that the accused is guilty. Nor, for that matter, is it in the best interests of the State to disclose their identity. There was a law. The law was broken. The law stipulated its penalty. My hands are tied.

Take her from where she stands, straight to the Island! There wall her up in a cell for life, with enough food to acquit ourselves of the taint of her blood.

WINSTON [*to the audience*].   Brothers and Sisters of the Land! I go now on my last journey. I must leave the light of day forever, for the Island, strange and cold, to be lost between life and death. So, to my grave, my everlasting prison, condemned alive to solitary death.

[*Tearing off his wig and confronting the audience as Winston, not Antigone.*]

Gods of our Fathers! My Land! My Home!

Time waits no longer. I go now to my living death, because I honoured those things to which honour belongs.

[*The two men take off their costumes and then strike their 'set'. They then come together and, as in the beginning, their hands come together to suggest handcuffs, and their right and left legs to suggest ankle-chains. They start running . . . John*]

*mumbling a prayer, and Winston a rhythm for their three-
legged run.
The siren wails.
Fade to blackout.*]

JUDITH BUTLER

Judith Butler is a contemporary philosopher best known for the conviction articulated in *Gender Trouble* (1990) that gender is not an
essential quality but an attribute that people acquire by performing
the behaviors and attitudes that are culturally ascribed to a particular gender. They are interested in the ways in which people who do
not conform to gender stereotypes can unsettle and remake prevail-
ing assumptions; in *Antigone's Claim: Kinship Between Life and
Death*, they explore this power in relation to Antigone, a figure who
refuses to behave like a conventional woman and whose family circumstances defy normative ideas about kinship and acceptable human
relations.

From Antigone's Claim†

Promiscuous Obedience

In George Steiner's study of the historical appropriations of
Antigone, he poses a controversial question he does not pursue:
What would happen if psychoanalysis were to have taken Antigone
rather than Oedipus as its point of departure?[1] Oedipus clearly has
his own tragic fate, but Antigone's fate is decidedly postoedipal.
Although her brothers are explicitly cursed by her father, does the
curse also work on her and, if so, through what furtive and implicit
means? The chorus remarks that something of Oedipus' fate is surely
working through her own, but what burden of history does she bear?
Oedipus comes to know who his mother and father are but finds that
his mother is also his wife. Antigone's father is her brother, since
they both share a mother in Jocasta, and her brothers are her neph-
ews, sons of her brother-father, Oedipus. The terms of kinship
become irreversibly equivocal. Is this part of her tragedy? Does this
equivocity of kinship lead to fatality?

---

† From *Antigone's Claim: Kinship Between Life and Death* (New York: Columbia University Press, 2000), pp. 57, 66–67, 69, 76–77, 80–82. Copyright © 2000 Columbia University Press. Reprinted with permission of Columbia University Press. Notes are by
  the editor of this Norton Critical Edition.
1. George Steiner, *Antigones* (New Haven: Yale UP, 1996), p. 18.

Antigone is caught in a web of relations that produce no coherent position within kinship. She is not, strictly speaking, outside kinship or, indeed, unintelligible. Her situation can be understood, but only with a certain amount of horror. * * *

* * *

The Antigonean revision of psychoanalytic theory might put into question the assumption that the incest taboo legitimates and normalizes kinship based in biological reproduction and the heterosexualization of the family. Although psychoanalysis has often insisted that normalization is invariably disrupted and foiled by what cannot be ordered by regulatory norms, it has rarely addressed the question of how new forms of kinship can and do arise on the basis of the incest taboo. From the presumption that one cannot—or ought not to—choose one's closest family members as one's lovers and marital partners, it does not follow that the bonds of kinship that *are* possible assume any particular form.

To the extent that the incest taboo contains its infraction within itself, it does not simply prohibit incest but rather sustains and cultivates incest as a necessary specter of social dissolution, a specter without which social bonds cannot emerge. Thus the prohibition against incest in the play *Antigone* requires a rethinking of prohibition itself, not merely as a negative or privative operation of power but as one that works precisely through proliferating through displacement the very crime that it bars. The taboo, and its threatening figuration of incest, delineates lines of kinship that harbor incest as their ownmost possibility, establishing "aberration" at the heart of the norm. Indeed, my question is whether it can also become the basis for a socially survivable aberration of kinship in which the norms that govern legitimate and illegitimate modes of kin association might be more radically redrawn.

Antigone says "brother," but does she mean "father"? She asserts her public right to grieve her kin, but how many of her kin does she leave ungrieved? Considering how many are dead in her family, is it possible that mother and father and repudiated sister and other brother are condensed there at the site of the irreproducible brother? What kind of psychoanalytic approach to Antigone's act would foreclose in advance any consideration of overdetermination at the level of the object? This equivocation at the site of the kinship term signals a decidedly postoedipal dilemma, one in which kin positions tend to slide into one another, in which Antigone is the brother, the brother is the father, and in which psychically, linguistically, this is true regardless of whether they are dead or alive; for anyone living in this slide of identifications, their fate will be an uncertain one, living within death, dying within life.

* * *

What is the contemporary voice that enters into the language of the law to disrupt its univocal workings? Consider that in the situation of blended families, a child says "mother" and might expect more than one individual to respond to the call. Or that, in the case of adoption, a child might say "father" and might mean both the absent phantasm she never knew as well as the one who assumes that place in living memory. The child might mean that at once, or sequentially, or in ways that are not always clearly disarticulated from one another. Or when a young girl comes to be fond of her stepbrother, what dilemma of kinship is she in? For a woman who is a single mother and has her child without a man, is the father still there, a spectral "position" or "place" that remains unfilled, or is there no such "place" or "position"? Is the father absent, or does this child have no father, no position, and no inhabitant? Is this a loss, which assumes the unfulfilled norm, or is it another configuration of primary attachment whose primary loss is not to have a language in which to articulate its terms? And when there are two men or two women who parent, are we to assume that some primary division of gendered roles organizes their psychic places within the scene, so that the empirical contingency of two same-gendered parents is nevertheless straightened out by the presocial psychic place of the Mother and Father into which they enter? Does it make sense on these occasions to insist that there are symbolic positions of Mother and Father that every psyche must accept regardless of the social form that kinship takes? Or is that a way of reinstating a heterosexual organization of parenting at the psychic level that can accommodate all manner of gender variation at the social level? * * *

* * *

In this light, then, it is perhaps interesting to note that Antigone, who concludes the oedipal drama, fails to produce heterosexual closure for that drama, and that this may intimate the direction for a psychoanalytic theory that takes Antigone as its point of departure. Certainly, she does not achieve another sexuality, one that is *not* heterosexuality, but she does seem to deinstitute heterosexuality by refusing to do what is necessary to stay alive for Haemon, by refusing to become a mother and a wife, by scandalizing the public with her wavering gender, by embracing death as her bridal chamber and identifying her tomb as a "deep dug home" (*kataskaphes oikesis*). If the love toward which she moves as she moves toward death is a love for her brother and thus, ambiguously, her father, it is also a love that can only be consummated by its obliteration, which is no consummation at all. As the bridal chamber is refused in life and pursued in death, it takes on a metaphorical status and, as metaphor, its conventional meaning is transmuted into a decidedly nonconventional one. If the tomb is the bridal chamber, and the tomb is chosen over marriage, then the tomb stands for the very destruction of marriage, and the term "bridal chamber" *(numpheion)* represents precisely the negation of its own possibility. The word destroys its object. In referring to the institution it names, the word performs the destruction of the institution. Is this not the operation of ambivalence in language that calls into question Antigone's sovereign control of her actions?

Although Hegel claims that Antigone acts with no unconscious, perhaps hers is an unconscious that leaves its trace in a different form, indeed that becomes readable precisely in her travails of referentiality. Her naming practice, for instance, ends up undoing its own ostensible aims. When she claims that she acts according to a law that gives her most precious brother precedence, and she appears to mean "Polyneices" by that description, she means more than she intends, for that brother could be Oedipus and it could be Eteocles, and there is nothing in the nomenclature of kinship that can successfully restrict its scope of referentiality to the single person, Polyneices. The chorus at one point seeks to remind her that she has more than one brother, but she continues to insist on the singularity and non-reproducibility of this term of kinship. In effect, she seeks to restrict the reproducibility of the word "brother" and to link it exclusively to the person of Polyneices, but she can do this only by displaying incoherence and inconsistency. The term continues to refer to those others she would exclude from its sphere of application, and she cannot reduce the nomenclature of kinship to nominalism. Her own language exceeds and defeats her stated desire, thereby manifesting something of what is beyond her intention, of what belongs to the particular fate that desire suffers in language. Thus she is unable to capture the radical singularity of her brother through a term that, by definition, must be transposable and reproducible in order to signify at all. Language thus disperses the desire she seeks to bind to him, cursing her, as it were, with a promiscuity she cannot contain.

*   *   *

Arendt,[2] of course, problematically distinguished the public and the private, arguing that in classical Greece the former alone was the sphere of the political, that the latter was mute, violent, and based

2. Hannah Arendt (1906–1975) was one of the most influential political philosophers of the twentieth century. The argument referred to here was developed primarily in *The Human Condition* (1958).

on the despotic power of the patriarch. * * * The slaves, women, and children, all those who were not property-holding males were not permitted into the public sphere in which the human was constituted through its linguistic deeds. Kinship and slavery thus condition the public sphere of the human and remain outside its terms. But is that the end of the story?

Who then is Antigone within such a scene, and what are we to make of her words, words that become dramatic events, performative acts? She is not of the human but speaks in its language. Prohibited from action, she nevertheless acts, and her act is hardly a simple assimilation to an existing norm. And in acting, as one who has no right to act, she upsets the vocabulary of kinship that is a precondition of the human, implicitly raising the question for us of what those preconditions really must be. She speaks within the language of entitlement from which she is excluded, participating in the language of the claim with which no final identification is possible. If she is human, then the human has entered into catachresis: we no longer know its proper usage. And to the extent that she occupies the language that can never belong to her, she functions as a chiasm within the vocabulary of political norms. If kinship is the precondition of the human, then Antigone is the occasion for a new field of the human, achieved through political catachresis, the one that happens when the less than human speaks as human, when gender is displaced, and kinship founders on its own founding laws. She acts, she speaks, she becomes one for whom the speech act is a fatal crime, but this fatality exceeds her life and enters the discourse of intelligibility as its own promising fatality, the social form of its aberrant, unprecedented future.

CRITICISM

MARK GRIFFITH

Antigone and Her Sister(s): Embodying Women in Greek Tragedy[†]

1. *Female Impersonation on the Tragic Stage*

The playwrights of the fifth century B.C.E. who competed each year in the Theater of Dionysus in Athens, with a series of three trage-dies and one satyr-play, were each assigned the same level of human resources: two or three actors, a chorus of twelve or fifteen, and a variable number of nonspeaking extras. All these cast members, like the playwright himself, were adult males. Thus there were no women's voices to be heard in the Theater of Dionysus. Yet over one-third of all speaking roles (including choruses) are female, and in several plays more than half the lines are delivered by women (e.g., Aeschylus *Suppliant Women, Choephoroi, Eumenides*; Sophocles *Electra*; Euripides *Medea, Andromache, Trojan Women*). The "voic-ing" and impersonation of women thus comprise a major part of the dramatic enterprise of Greek tragedy.

Playing female roles was not in itself a specialized activity, for it seems to have been expected of all actors and chorus members. Actors often switched back and forth between male and female roles within the same play; and likewise the chorus members would be required during the course of each trilogy to take on three quite dif-ferent choral identities, at least one of which would usually be female. (In the fourth play, of course, the chorus members were always satyrs.)

As far as we can tell, no particular physical or vocal characteris-tics were preferred for actors and choreuts,[1] nor was the vocal train-ing very specialized (in contrast to the theatrical traditions of, for example, India or Japan), though it became more so as the fifth century progressed and acting turned into more of a virtuoso per-formance in its own right, especially in the lyric modes. For the most part, male and female characters are found in tragic dialogue to employ the same metrical and linguistic forms, and the small dif-ferences of expression that can be observed are mostly quite subtle

[†] From *Making Silence Speak: Women's Voices in Greek Literature and Society*, ed. André Lardinois and Laura McClure (Princeton: Princeton University Press, 2001), pp. 117–36. Reprinted with permission. Notes are by the editor of this Norton Critical Edition. The author's notes and some Greek phrases have been omitted. Plays referenced in this essay are abbreviated as follows: Aeschylus: *Ag.=Agamemnon, Cho.=Choephoroi* or *Libation Bearers, Pers.=Persians*; Sophocles: *Trach.=Trachiniae* or *Women of Trachis*; Euripides: *Hipp.=Hippolytus, IA=Iphigenia in Aulis, Med.=Medea*.
1. Performers in the Chorus.

and sporadic: no sharp or consistent differentiation was made in the mode of delivery. References in tragedy to "sharp, high" tones often denote intensity and distress, but not necessarily femininity; and male actors and choruses seem not to have made any thorough-going attempt to speak or sing "like" women (i.e., by adopting a falsetto delivery, or modifying their voices in any systematic way). In Aristophanes' *Thesmophoriazusae* 86–278, for example, the poet and actor involved in constructing and playing female tragic roles (Agathon and Mnesilochus) are clearly expected to adopt distinctive attitudes and movements, along with their costumes, and to sing cer-tain kinds of songs; but the advice "Be sure you do a good job of being a woman with your voice!" (267–68) does not indicate how specifically this is to be achieved. In lyrics, distinctions between male and female expressions and modes of delivery could be more sharply drawn, but even here we cannot be sure how realistically the intonation and mannerisms of Greek or foreign mourners, princesses, slave attendants, goddesses, and other female charac-ters were represented onstage.

In general, "female impersonation" relied more heavily on gesture, gait, dance step, and bearing, and on changes of costume, than on distinctively feminine voice or language. An expert actor could change "character" in just a few seconds: masks and wigs concealed the actors' beards, and the long-sleeved, ankle-length garments con-ventionally worn for the leading roles, in addition to conveying the appropriate opulence and dignity of the Bronze Age[2] heroes and heroines of myth, would also cover hairy, muscular arms and legs. Thus, overall, the most distinct features of any role, female or male, were conveyed in the first place through means other than the voice: a Nurse, or Queen, or Slave Chorus was recognizable even before a word was spoken, from mask, costume, posture, and movement.

Training in use of the body (with or without the voice) in perfor-mance of this or that social role, whether in play or in ritual (or even in athletics and war), was second nature to most Greeks. Different age and gender groups were distinguished by their own formations, songs, and dances, and in some cases their rituals also involved imperson-ation of one kind or another as part of the group's process of self-definition and self-presentation. Athenians were thus quite accustomed to recognizing, and selectively adopting, various conventional patterns of behavior, or performativities, appropriate to this or that context and role, each with its distinct and distinctive semiotic code.

Indeed, rites of passage and initiation, athletic and military train-ing, distinctions of sex/gender, class, and ethnicity, would be empty

2. The much earlier period (around 1750–1200 B.C.E.) during which the events of Greek mythology were believed to have taken place.

and ineffectual without such systems of linguistic, aesthetic, and bodily citation and (re)inforcement. Girls' and women's, boys' and men's choruses must not present themselves in the same ways, or they could not succeed in instituting their members into their proper social roles, and investing them with all the entitlements and restrictions to which they are due.

Athenian tragedy draws upon many of these choral and ritual performativities, even as it assimilates them to its own consistent and authoritative conventions and style. Thus, while iambic trimeters and lyric strophes impose their unique and inviolable stamp on every utterance (Persian Messenger or Theban King, slave Nurse or Bacchante Chorus, they all speak good Attic Greek[3]), nonetheless the tragic plots present a strikingly diverse array of contexts and "characters." For this reason, tragedy may often preserve, or even reinvent, particular performative modes that were otherwise becoming socially obsolete or suspect; and this may be one of the reasons why women, whose public roles in democratic Athens were very limited, except in the sphere of religious practice, are given such prominence in the stage drama of the fifth century.

Just as tragedy employs an array of conventional masks to represent different (recurring) "types" of character (King, Old Tutor, Nurse, Young Princess, Blind Prophet, etc.), so we might look for a repertoire of associated performativities, incorporating specific details of idiolect, gesture, costume, musical modes, and choreography, by means of which a playwright could construct for each of his characters and choruses their proper person and "voice," a voice distinguished (if at all), not by pitch, regional/class accent, dialect, or even timbre, but by rhetoric and patterns of speech.

So, what distinctions do we observe in our surviving tragic texts? What specific performative conventions, verbal mannerisms, and rhetorical strategies (in addition to the use of grammatically feminine word-endings) could be employed by the playwrights to assist their actors in representing women onstage? Can we identify particular types of utterance, linguistic usages or styles of delivery, modes of argument or self-presentation, that are marked as exclusively, or primarily, "feminine"? Did/do "women" have (a) distinctive voice(s) in Athenian tragedy?

The answer (predictably) is: Yes and no—but perhaps more "no" than "yes." It is true that certain kinds of emotive expression are usually reserved for female (or "barbarian") characters: in particular, ritual lamentation (*goos, thrēnos, kommos*) and actor's "monody" (solo aria). Such highly colored expressions of emotion, though they might once have been acceptable Attic practice, and were still to be

---

3. Belonging to Attica, the region that included Athens.

found in several non-Attic Greek communities, were felt to be extravagant and unmanly by classical Athenian standards. Likewise, certain kinds of agonized exclamation are largely confined to women—or to men who are explicitly said to be suffering from debilitating, or Orientalizing and "feminine," loss of self-control. Yet these distinctions are not hard and fast: a Prometheus, or Philoctetes, or Heracles may "sing" (or "wail"?) briefly, when he is to be imagined as being in the most extreme throes of victimization and agony; and when the young Argive prince Orestes joins the Asian slave-chorus and his own sister, Electra, in a wild, extended lament and invocation of their dead father (Aesch. *Cho.* 306–478), it is impossible at times to distinguish his male voice from the two female voices with which he is alternating, so univocally are their words, meters, self-representations, and rhetorics merged and integrated. Thus the (collective, nongendered) voice of "aristocratic family lament" and "children's cry for vengeance," in this case at least, proves stronger than the distinctive strains of "female utterance"; or, to put this another way, a man may—under circumstances of exceptional stress—have access to a language, or a "voice," normally, or selectively, restricted to women and/or foreigners. If a man gives in too completely to this mode of utterance, he may indeed run the risk of being seen as effeminized (as Heracles does at Soph. *Trach.* 1070–75, or Xerxes in Aesch. *Pers.*). Yet, in the artificial world of the Theater, forbidden practices from past eras, or repressed fantasies normally excluded from public male discourse, might surface and find exciting and (temporarily) legitimate expression.

*   *   *

The Greeks themselves often asserted that women should be judged by different behavioral, moral, musical, and verbal standards from men. In general, a woman's "virtue" (*aretē*) was often declared to be different from a man's, just as a slave's is different from a master's; and words—especially certain kinds of assertive, defiant, courageous, independent-minded words—that would be fine and admirable for a man to utter might be improper, foolish, even outrageous for a woman.

Some of the most distinctively female patterns of speech in tragedy are obvious enough: lyric expressions of fear and grief; prayers to the gods for help; other ritual formulations, such as supplication, prophecies, curses, and various perlocutionary chants of damage or benefit; references to domestic activities such as making and washing clothes, fetching water, making offerings, taking care of young children; descriptions of the miseries of slavery and loss of homeland and family; references to the intimate relations between child and mother or between sexual partners—all these are usually found coming from female characters rather than male. * * * Accordingly, in Sophocles *Antigone*, it is the conventionally "feminine" Ismene, not Creon or Haemon himself—nor the "unfeminine" Antigone— who refers to the bond of affection between Haemon and Antigone (*Ant.* 570): male references to the power of Eros usually characterize it as an affliction or disease.

Another characteristic associated by the Greeks more with women than with men is silence; and a silence that would be shameful or cowardly in a man might conventionally be thought to confer an ideal air of "modesty" and "good sense" upon a woman. Indeed, one of the most distinctive signs of "femininity" on the tragic stage is failure to speak at all (Sophocles' Iole, Aeschylus' Iphigenia or Helen, Euripides' veiled Alcestis), or inability to keep on speaking— whether this silencing is brought about by intimidation, by rhetorical convention, or by physical removal (Sophocles' Chrysothemis or Tecmessa, Euripides' Phaedra or Alcestis, Aeschylus' Cassandra, Io, or—ultimately—Clytemnestra).

By contrast, tragedy presents a select number of female characters whose "masculine" speech arouses the horror and/or admiration of other characters and critics alike. Among these we must count Aeschylus' Clytemnestra, Sophocles' Electra and Antigone, and Euripides' Medea. In all four of these cases, it is striking that we find the character described both as typically or exaggeratedly "womanly," and as shamefully bold and "manly." Aeschylus' Clytemnestra, for example, even as she confirms her reputation for having a "male-counselling, expectant heart" (*Ag.* 11) by hacking her husband to death, and subsequently by calling for "a man-slaying axe" to deal with her avenging son (*Cho.* 889), is also criticized by the male chorus for her female flights of fancy, and later reveals her "feminine" susceptibility to sexual temptation: "No expectation of fear steps in my house, as long as Aegisthus warms the fire on my hearth" (*Ag.* 1434–35; cf. *Cho.* 893). She also mentions (effusively, but with some irony) her dependency on her husband (*Ag.* 855–913), and her maternal concern for her daughter (genuine) and son (perhaps feigned: *Cho.* 691–99; cf. 737–43). Likewise, her eerily knowledgeable vision of distant events at Troy gives her a "prophetic" air (not unlike, e.g., Theonoe's in Eur. *Helen*), and her obvious relish for deception conforms to the feminine stereotype established with/by Hesiod's Pandora.

Medea similarly combines a "masculine" determination to exact revenge on her enemies at any cost with a passionate jealousy directed against her husband's new bride, and an explicit commitment to the traditional "womanly" resources of deception and trickery (*Med.* 393–409):

> I myself, taking a sword, even if I end up being killed,
> will kill them; I will proceed to resolute and bold action.
> For nobody—by the Mistress whom I revere above all
> and have chosen as my ally, Hecate,
> who resides in the inner chamber of my house—
> none of them will hurt my heart and escape unharmed. . . .
> Come Medea . . . , now the test is of your courage;
> . . . You must not let yourself be laughed at
> as a result of this Corinthian marriage of Jason's,
> when you yourself are born from a noble father, and
>   from the Sun.
> You know what is required; and furthermore, we are
>   women—
> most helpless for good, but the cleverest architects of
>   all evils.

And as the play proceeds, we see her steel herself to murder her own children, in a nightmarish combination of cold-blooded rage (at their father) and tender concern (for the children's future without her—and for their very survival).

Some of the most agonizing and introspective scenes of indecision in tragedy are focused on women: in addition to Medea herself, we may point especially to Phaedra (Eur. *Hipp.*), Iphigenia (Eur. *IA*), and Deianira (Soph. *Trach.*). That is not to say that men never experience such moments, but the most searching explorations of impossibly conflicted inner feelings (as opposed to conflicting societal expectations) tend to be attributed to women.

✳   ✳   ✳

2. *The Three Women of* Antigone

Sophocles' *Antigone* provides a rich and instructive sampling of the range of possibilities for women's voices in tragedy, exemplifying, on the one hand, the multiplicity of "female" attitudes and modes of expression available, and on the other, the impossibility of isolating any particular quality as belonging exclusively or quintessentially to the category "woman," or "female." Woman as daughter, as sister, as bride, as wife, as mother: each has a distinct performativity and rhetoric, some of them overlapping, others diverging and even contradicting one another. We can learn much from tracing the interweaving strands of these discourses.

Three women appear in the play: the two sisters, Antigone and Ismene, and Creon's wife, Eurydice (mother of Haemon). Each of these three speaks with a distinctly, even radically, different voice; furthermore, in addition to their own words, each also has her speech and behavior imagined and described in her absence, or even in her presence, by other speakers in the play. Thus, in each case, "woman" is constructed as a speaking subject in conjunction with, or in opposition to, other characters, male and female.

The opening lines present the two sisters in close contact and collusion; but this closeness is almost immediately ruptured. Symptomatic of this troubled closeness—and of the uncomfortable and intricate family history and relations that produced it—is the frequent use of the dual[4] ("we two," "our two brothers," etc.: 2–3, 13–14, 21, 50, 55–57, 58, 61–62), and of the *auto-* root, whose associations of "selfsame, very own, mutual" can be positive ("very own sister") or negative ("self-inflicted," "incestuous": 1, 49–52, 55–57; later 306–7, 511–13, 863–65, 900, 915, 1172–75, 1315). As the scene progresses (1–99), Antigone in particular begins to employ the first- and second-person pronouns and verb-endings increasingly in opposition to one another (31–32, 37–38, 45–46, 71–72, 76–77, 80–81, 83, etc.), and even to threaten Ismene with "hatred" (86, 92–93). The siblings' hoped-for identity of interests and persons thus disintegrates into bitter opposition, and this is reflected in the contrast between the speech patterns of the unassertive, reasonable, and conventional-minded Ismene, and those of the uncompromising and single-minded Antigone. Antigone's speech favors blunt direct questions (2–3, 9–10) and future indicative statements (esp. 37, 46, 71–77, 80–81, 93), shorter and less complicated sentences, often enjambed[5] (especially in the staccato phrases of her indignant rejection of Ismene at 69–77); and she prefers simple vocabulary and insistent repetition (2–3, 32, 73, 93–94; negatives at 4–6). Ismene speaks in more elaborate periods (esp. 49–68), with more ornate diction, preferring potential and conditional utterance and a greater degree of generalization (61–62, 67–68, 92): she is seeking to establish a measured and balanced basis for decision-making, a set of principles that will make it possible for the remains of their family to recover themselves after this latest calamity, while Antigone sees only what lies directly before them—a body, her brother's body, to be buried: "Do you know . . . ? Have you heard . . . ? Or are you unaware . . . ?" (*Ant.* 2, 9–10); "Be what it seems best to you! I shall bury him" (*Ant.* 71–72).

This directness of expression continues to characterize Antigone's speech throughout the play; and it is further emphasized at times by a heavy use of negative particles and sarcastic dismissals of the suggestions of others. Her language is contrasted not only with Ismene's, but also to an even greater degree with Creon's frequent

4. Greek has special "dual" forms to refer to not one or many but two people or things.
5. Continuing over to the next line.

*gnōmai*⁶ and generalizations, preference for the abstract over the concrete, and extensive use of analogies, metaphors, and similes, all of which characterize him as one who thinks in terms of rules, of hierarchies, and of predictable and controllable orders. Several critics have remarked on this contrast of speech patterns, and some have seen it as conforming to a more general gender-based distinction: men are more logical and abstract, women more intuitive and concrete (or, as a refinement of this, the male-dominated sociopolitical world requires more absolute, generalizable rules, while women are usually called upon to make their moral decisions in contexts that require more particular and provisional judgments, often made *ad hominem*⁷). From another (less overtly gender-charged) perspective, Creon is viewed as representing men's (or humans'?) futile attempts at ruling the world by their own laws, extrapolations, and institutions, whereas Antigone speaks and acts in the name of higher (divine) truths incapable of rational exposition and capable only of direct or intuitive apprehension.

Some such distinction is confirmed by the differing usages of words of "knowing," "learning," and "being aware": Creon, along with the other male characters (especially Haemon and the chorus), constantly harps on the need for "intelligence, good sense, planning" (*phronein, gnōmē, bouleuma, euboulia, nous,* etc.) and "learning, understanding" (*manthanein*), whereas for Antigone to "know" (*eidenai, epistasthai*) seems to involve a more immediate, less intellectual state of awareness, or "certainty" (18, 89, 447–48, 460, 521; 471–72, 480):

> [CREON:]   Did you know (*eidēstha*) it had been decreed not to do this?
> [ANT.:]   I knew (*eidē*) . . . ; how could I not? It was clear to all. (447–48)

> [ANT.:]   I knew I was going to die; of course I knew (*exēidē*) (460)

> [CHO.:]   She does not know (*ouk epistatai*) [how] to yield to troubles. (472)

Yet before we assign Antigone's mentality and language too confidently to the category of "female," against Creon's "male," we should recall the ways in which her speeches earlier clashed with Ismene's milder and less aggressive style and diction. Each sister thus speaks in a manner that is characterized as distinctively "female"—yet, as we have seen, their respective manners of speech are sharply differentiated from one another. Indeed, as Antigone asserts her

6. Statements of conventional wisdom.
7. In reference to a particular person.

intention of going off to bury the body, in defiance of Creon's edict, Ismene reminds her (*Ant.* 58–62):

> So look and consider, now the two of us are left on our own,
> how miserably we will perish, if we violate the law
> and transgress the vote and authority of the rulers.
> We must bear in mind that we were born women,
> so we must not try to fight against men.

This is sensible advice; nobody could blame a young woman for submitting thus to an official edict, however harsh—nobody, that is, except Antigone (*Ant.* 69–70): "I won't tell you what to do. In fact, even if you should want / to do it now, I wouldn't want to let you join me in carrying it out!" In her anger at Ismene's caution and reserve, she rejects her completely, a reaction that is repeated later in the play. Thus her subsequent claim, "I was born to share in love, not in hate" (523), is seen to have a very limited application—her "love" is for her father and her brother, but it extends no further; indeed, it is converted into hate as soon as it encounters resistance (86, 93, etc.). Despite Ismene's subsequent offer to join her in opposition to Creon, and risk death along with her, Antigone continues to reject her (536–60), and later describes herself as "the last" of Oedipus' family (895), as if Ismene no longer existed. And indeed, Ismene soon fades completely from the scene, and from our consciousness (she is never mentioned again after line 771, the point at which Creon relents and agrees to punish only Antigone). Her role has been to articulate "normal," conventional female attitudes and expectations, in order to throw into even sharper relief Antigone's extreme and unconventional behavior and views. And once Antigone's portrait is complete, and her fate sealed, Ismene has no further function to perform.

Antigone herself is one of the most discussed and most admired figures of Greek literature, at least since the nineteenth century. A young woman who chooses to die for her brother, in lone resistance to an oppressive state government; a woman sentenced to a dark and solitary "marriage to death," who takes her fate in her own hands and commits suicide, to be joined in death by her youthful fiancé; a woman who rejects human (institutional) authority in the name of divine law; yet at the same time one whose incestuous origin reasserts itself in her privileging of father and brother over sister or potential husband and children—she is a complex and contradictory figure. To some, she has appeared a passionate, loving sister and daughter, inspired by commitment to a higher and more perfect set of ideals than anyone else around her; to others, she is an inflexible but confused rebel, or fatal victim of a family's curse. Her voice is unusually individual and insistent, and it carries with it associations

that are both manly and feminine, dutiful and transgressive, enlight-
ened and narrow, typical and unique.

This is at least in part because Antigone's—and her family's—
identity is itself so peculiar: "Oh common, self-sistered head of
Ismene" (1). All four of the brothers and sisters, and their father,
too, are indeed "common and self/same-siblinged," an identity to
which Antigone will sacrifice anything else in the world, including
her own life. For her devotion to her *philoi* ("loved ones, nearest
and dearest") knows no limits: "In love, I shall lie with him, with
my loved one, having committed a holy crime." (73–74). The "crime"
to which she refers here, with consciously scornful paradox, is vio-
lation of Creon's edict forbidding burial of her brother's body. In
this devotion to kin, and her resolute observance of proper funeral
rites (washing a family member's body, wailing and lamenting over
it), Antigone is performing a characteristic and proper female role;
and she insists that by this action she is recognizing and honoring a
universal obligation to the gods below (450–60). The fact that this
brings her into collision with the legitimate political authorities and
jeopardizes her own prospects of marriage, and even of life itself,
does not deter her (*Ant.* 461–67):

> If I am to die before my time, I count that as a profit;
> Anyone who lives as I do, amidst many evils,
> doesn't this man (*hode*) derive profit by dying?
> So it is no pain for me to meet this end;
> but if I had left my own brother's corpse unburied,
> at that I would have felt pain.

Late in the play, when she is about to be led off to her living tomb,
Antigone stipulates that she would not have acted so for a husband
or child, but only for a brother, since, with their parents dead, he is
irreplaceable (900–912). Some critics (especially those who take
Antigone's earlier claims as representing "family" against "state")
have seen this argument as a sign of youthful or "feminine" inconsistency, or loss of nerve, or special pleading, evidence that Antigone
is not in fact acting on rational principles, but out of a semi-articulate
spirit of sisterly devotion or divine enlightenment. But her words
here are not inconsistent with her former claims—merely more nar-
rowly specific about her absolute commitment to natal family. In that
respect, she is voicing (and enacting) a preference, or a contradiction,
that lies at the heart of Greek gender relations, yet rarely finds overt
expression: to which of her two families does a woman (bride, mother)
owe stronger allegiance, that of her parents (including her siblings),
or that of her husband (including her children and in-laws)? If exog-
amy (the exchange of women between households through marriage) is designed ideally to enable families to develop and extend

their kinship ties, this institution brings with it an inherent conflict of interest—a conflict that men do not face, since they are never required to leave one household (their father's) to take up residence in another (their spouse's).

Thus the deep-seated male fear that a wife will betray her "new" family out of loyalty to her "old" one finds its confirmation in Antigone's defiant statements, which amount to a resounding rejection of the institution of marriage itself. This rejection finds repeated expression in her observation (echoed by others) that her living entombment constitutes a "marriage to Death": her rocky "tomb" is her "bridal chamber underground," and she will be (re)united there with her dead parents, and above all with her beloved brother. These phrases, and the haunting spectacle of her being led off to her new "bridal chamber" (891, *numpheion*, etc.), underline the paradoxical character of a woman who is at the same time the most loyal daughter and the most impossible bride imaginable. Antigone never mentions Haemon; and she remains silent when his name and their planned marriage are discussed by Ismene and Creon (561–76). It is not Antigone but her more conventionally feminine sister who alludes to their "attachment" (570, *hērmosmena*) and cries out on behalf of "dearest Haemon" (572); and Creon recognizes this in his retort ("You and your [talk of] marriage are causing me pain," 573). It is no coincidence that the only character who addresses or refers to Antigone as "woman" (*gynē*) in the play is Creon: to the others, she is always "child" (*pais*), "girl" (*neanis* or *korē*), "bride" (*numphē*), or "maiden" (*parthenos*), or else plain "Antigone." *Gynē* implies "adult woman" or "wife," but it is also the regular term used in binary opposition to *anēr* ("man"), and therefore the most suitable for misogynistic insults; hence Creon's repeated use of the term in his confrontation with Haemon (649, 651, 678, 680, 740, 746, 756; cf. 694).

Just as Ismene earlier characterizes Antigone's speech and behavior as unfeminine, Creon, too, accuses her of usurping "the man's" role (*Ant*. 480–85):

> She knew how to commit outrage (*hubris*) then,
> when she overstepped the established laws;
> and this is a second outrage (*hubris*), on top of her action,
> that she boasts about what she did, and exults in it.
> Certainly I am no longer the man—she is the man,
> if authority (*kratē*) is to be overturned like this with impunity.

By conventional male—and political—standards, it is a serious "outrage" (*hubris*) to flout the law and perform a forbidden act, especially out in public, on the open plain; but for Creon it seems almost more "outrageous" that she "voices so vehemently and gleefully" (*epauchein kai gelān*, 483) her responsibility. By this point in their confrontation, he has been riled by her dismissive tone and her scornful remarks (e.g., "If I seem to you to be acting foolishly, I can hardly be found guilty of foolishness by a fool!" 469–70). But even in her first words to him, neutral as they are, she has transgressed (*Ant.* 442–43):

> [CR.:]   Do you say, or do you deny, that you did this deed?
> [ANT.:]   I say that I did it; I don't deny it.

To see a woman stand her ground, look up at the city's chief officer, and thus break silence; to hear her lay claim publicly to an act of direct opposition to political authority; this can only happen in the Theater. Yet, unlike Clytemnestra's or Medea's stridently defiant claims, or Deianira's or Phaedra's self-accusatory disclaimers, Antigone's simple assertion of responsibility carries a disconcerting air of absolute authority.

The third female voice in this play is that of Creon's wife, Eurydice. She says very little. In fact, her speaking role is the shortest (except for Aeschylus' Pylades) of any named character in Greek tragedy (1183–91), though a few more words and cries of hers are later reported by a Messenger (1302–5). Her chief function is to receive the news of Haemon's death, and then by her suicide to become another component in Creon's downfall and final misery. Yet, short though her part is, it is in several respects typical of many female roles in tragedy, and illuminating both for what it (she) says, and for the way(s) in which she falls silent. Here is Eurydice's entire speech (*Ant.* 1183–91):

> All you citizens, I heard the news
> as I was coming up to the doorway,
> to go and present prayers to the goddess, Pallas Athena;
> I happened to be loosening the bolt of the gate,
> when the voice of disaster to our house struck right
>   through my ears.
> I fainted in terror, and lay there in front of my servants,
>   struck dumb.
> But tell me again what the news was;
> I am not inexperienced in disasters; I will listen to this, too.

The opening apology (why is she here at all, in public, out of the house? cf. 18–19), the allusive reference to previous miseries, and the steeling of herself to take in the grimmest news possible (the death of her only surviving son) are all common motifs from female characters in tragedy. What is unusual here, and highly effective, is Sophocles' decision to have Eurydice rush from the stage without a word, once she has heard the full news of Haemon's death (*Ant.* 1244–45):

[CHO.:]   What would you guess? The woman has gone back
     inside again, before saying anything, good or bad.

The Messenger and chorus debate for a few lines what to make of
Eurydice's sudden departure (*Ant.* 1253–56):

We shall soon know whether she is concealing
something hidden in her raging heart,
if we go inside the house; you are right:
there is a weight of danger even in excessive silence.

Their suspicions are well founded: she has killed herself—but not
before uttering a final curse on her husband (*Ant.* 1301–5):

Pierced by the sharp sword, near the altar, . . .
she closed her darkening eyes, bewailing (*kōkūsāsa*)
the empty marriage bed of Megareus,
who had died in the past, and now Haemon, too;
and finally she sang out evil-doings (*kakās praxeis
   ephumnēsāsa*)
against you, the child-killer.

This woman is defined entirely by her role as wife and mother, and
when both of her sons have been taken from her (both, it seems, as
a result of something her husband did), she has nothing to live for.
Her anger, despair, and bitterness are channeled into two violent,
yet typically "female," acts (an act and a speech act): suicide and
curses on her husband. Like Antigone, she succeeds in hurting
Creon even in and after her death; and like her, in so acting/
speaking, she commands the strongest sympathy and approval from
the theater audience.

Nonetheless, for all of the powerful impact of Eurydice's brief
appearance and death, and all of Ismene's value as a foil to Antigone
(and as a representative of "normalcy," too, amidst so much extravagant and misguided behavior), it is Antigone's voice that resonates
most strongly from the play (at least in modern times), her person-
ality that makes the most memorable and disturbing impression on
the theater audience and the reader. So it is with Antigone that we
should conclude. Is hers a voice of resistance, of potential libera-
tion? In opposing a misguided political regime, breaking with conventional stereotypes of female submission and obedience, and
asserting her own ineradicable right—as a human being, regardless
of gender or status—to carry out such a universal obligation as burial
of kin, does she not succeed in challenging and overthrowing Creon's short-sighted and bigoted version of male supremacy and political expediency? And if so, isn't her voice thereby proven to be "truer,"
or "higher," than Ismene's, the voice that recommended caution,

compromise, and accommodation? If so, is it more—or less—
"feminine" than Ismene's?

Or are we to conclude that it was Antigone's own transgressive
and uncompromising ("unfeminine"?) temper that brought about the
fatal collision and catastrophe ("Your own self-willed temper
destroyed you," 875), together with her obsessive devotion to father
and brother, to the exclusion of other "normal" objects of devotion,
such as sister or future husband? Or (extending this possibility a
little further) is her position and behavior to be explained entirely
in terms of her incestuous origin, from that archetypally Oedipal
family in which the "daughter" can only imagine herself as loving
(and "lying with") her own father and brother—and therefore must
be consigned (must consign herself) to death?

During the course of the play, Antigone embodies all these possibilities, or performativities. Her voice speaks loudly, piercingly, and
effectively—but not univocally. Indeed, Athenian tragedy provides
an extraordinarily richly textured, and often contradictory, babble
of rival voices, as the various characters are embodied, masked, and
endowed with speech by their authors and actors. Dramatic impersonation is a form of contestation and pretension, of laying claim to
and trying out voices and roles that are not normally our own.
Antigone's voice, and Ismene's, and even Eurydice's, are allowed to
formulate queries and complaints, propose and violate norms, cite
and blur this performativity and that, and thereby bring about
shocking and edifying results. This process appears to have been
useful, even necessary, to Sophocles and his male fellow-citizens,
for representing and critiquing their society, as it is, as it might be, as
it is imagined to be, for Dionysiac tragedy was the most admired
and highly valued cultural event of the Athenian year.

What did Athenian men believe, or fantasize, about their daughters,
their mothers, their sisters, their wives, their slaves? What did they
want to believe? What did they fear? The roles that the tragedians
wrote to be played out in the Theater by themselves and their fellow
actors and choreuts remind the audience constantly how fragile and
tormented the family relations are out of which they all come, and
within which they all continue to function, even as they pursue their
careers within the city as soldiers, competitors, and politicians. By
giving voice—outspoken voice—to any and all of those family members, including the ones who normally keep quiet, stay out of public
view, and "mind their own business," they allow unconscious anxi-
eties to surface, unspoken contradictions to be stated, and unmen-
tionable issues to be aired. Tragic "women" are especially good
for that: for while real-life Athenian women would not dream of
talking about (let alone acting on) the kinds of conflicts and fantasies

that these plays explore—and conversely there are certain things that men in real life are not expected to say, certain sounds they cannot be allowed to make, if they are to remain sufficiently different and distinct from women—in the Theater the power of disguise, and the license of impersonation, allows extraordinary liberties to be taken.

As for us, nowadays, what we end up making of these impersonated "women," how we evaluate their words and performativities within the drama that each inhabits, is open to discussion: it is up to us. Certainly, no neatly defined portrait of "woman" emerges (from this play, or from any other—or from Greek tragedy overall): no comfortable confirmation of preexisting distinctions of gender, of predictable mannerisms of speech, or of the natural divisions between male and female. For the term "woman" is too clumsy an umbrella for too many separate categories (daughter, sister, virgin, bride, wife, mother, princess, captive, etc.), whose several duties and expectations cannot be expected to cohere tidily—nor to separate themselves out conveniently and invariably (essentially) from those of son, brother, youth, husband, and father. The urge (within some of the play's characters, and perhaps within many members of Sophocles' audience, as with some readers in our own day) to find and maintain distinctions, to listen for the authentic voice of "woman," and to seize on particular formulations and enunciations as proof of inherent difference (whether inferiority, or superiority, or mysterious complementarity) is found to lead in circles: women do not all speak alike (any more than men do); and they do not always speak as "women"—though sometimes their words will be misheard, or heard in a particular way, or not heard at all, precisely because all that is heard, or noticed, is a "woman's" voice.

KIRK ORMAND

Creon the Family Man[†]

Many critics have argued that Creon represents the interests of the state, as opposed to those of the family. It is not always easy, however, to determine exactly where the family leaves off and the city begins in fifth-century Athens. More importantly, as we shall see,

---

† From *Exchange and the Maiden: Marriage in Sophoclean Tragedy* (Austin: University of Texas Press 1999), pp. 80–86. Copyright © 1999 by the University of Texas Press. Reprinted by permission of the publisher. Notes are by the editor of this Norton Critical Edition. The author's notes and quotations in Greek have been omitted.

Creon clearly does have an interest in the family—it is merely a question of how he defines that family. A key scene is the argument between Creon and his son Haemon. Once Antigone has been captured, Haemon approaches his father to plead for her release. Creon sees this exchange in explicitly familial terms. He begins his conversation with Haemon with a question:

> Child, I hope you have not come raving mad at your father,
> having heard the final vote concerning your soon-to-be bride?
> Or am I your *philos* no matter what I do? (632–34)

Creon is, for whatever reason, seriously concerned about his relations with his son. Moreover, he describes those relations as a form of *philia*.[1] As standard readings of this play would have it, Creon defines *philoi* in terms of service to the state, Antigone in terms of family ties. This is not strictly true. As Haemon approaches, Creon worries about Haemon's treatment of him as a father. Admittedly, he will use his model of the family shortly to describe successful civic government (659–60), but that does not erase the familial concern present here.

Haemon seems to recognize Creon's concern, and answers his questions with a little speech that should please his father:

> Father, I am yours. And you give me straight advice,
> which I, for my part, will follow.
> For no marriage will be worth more to me
> than to be guided by your sound leadership. (635–38)

He explicitly states his dedication, not to Creon as ruler of Thebes, but to his father as an advisor in the matter of marriage. And this is a role that Creon takes seriously. In a generalizing statement a few lines later, he gives Haemon advice on choosing a bride:

> Do not ever, child, throw away your mind for pleasure
> on account of a woman, knowing that
> this becomes a cold embrace,
> an evil wife sleeping with you in the house. (648–51)

Obviously Creon has Antigone in mind. He may be misjudging her, but it seems foolish to doubt that he genuinely thinks she would make a bad wife. We see the same motivation in his response to Ismene's question (above): ("I hate evil wives for sons," 571). The drift of Creon's words, moreover, implies that Antigone's danger lies in a sexual desirability. As a *parankalisma* ("embrace") in line 650,

---

1. A term for ties between people, which may take the form of kinship, friendship, political alliance, or love. People in relations of *philia* are *philoi*.

she is clearly figured as a bedmate, a notion further implied by
suneunos ("bedmate") in the next line. Creon wants particularly to
warn Haemon against her false physical charms (false, since she will
be a "cold" embrace). What is especially bad about such a wife, as
the language in 650–51 shows, is that she is *in the house*, in a privi-
leged and intimate position. Above all else, then, Creon fears that
the desirability of Antigone will create discord in his relations with
Haemon. It is crucial, therefore, that he set the father–son bond as
prior in importance to that of (potential) husband and wife.

We know that Demosthenes[2] found Creon's opening speech to be
a model for a good ruler. Creon's advice on marriage, too, probably
struck a responsive chord. Athenian men were evidently concerned
with the possibility that sexually desirable women could sway a
young man's senses and cloud his judgment. Isaeus[3] warns, for
example, that young men who lack self-control might be led astray
by the wrong sort of woman. The mistake that such men may make
is in agreeing to marry sexually desirable women even though their
citizenship is questionable, and their class is not suitable for the men
marrying them. Ultimately, then, a woman's sexual attractions are
a threat to the state, whether the danger is in falsifying citizenship
(as is the case in Isaeus 3) or merely in undermining masculine
authority (as is the case in the *Antigone*). Creon is not anti-family,
any more than is Isaeus. Rather, Creon sees the family as necessary
for the city, but also as potentially destructive of order within the
city. If the husband chooses a woman for a wife because of her sexual desirability, rather than in accord with his father's wishes, then
the formation of a new family becomes a threat to the masculine
hierarchy. In other words, Antigone presents a double threat here.
As the person who buried Polyneices, she undermines Creon's
political authority, but as an unmarried, potentially seductive woman,
she has access to a momentary subjectivity and could subvert Creon's
family.

The question, then, is what sort of family Creon envisions. At his
most extreme, Creon resembles Heracles in the *Trachiniae*. He sees
his family as a succession of men, for whom women present a perhaps necessary but dangerous and suspect mediation. At times (as
above) he merely tries to control that mediation. In other places, he
tells a story of civilization that excludes women altogether. In fact,
in his next speech Creon will borrow from Hesiod[4] to draw his ideal
image of society:

---

2. A prominent politician and orator.
3. Author of speeches delivered during legal trials.
4. Eighth-century B.C.E. poet, whose *Works and Days* explains how to live a virtuous life as
   a hardworking farmer.

> For this reason men pray to sow
> obedient offspring to have in the house
> so that they will ward off enemies by doing them harm,
> and will honor friends equally with their father.
> And whoever begets unhelpful children,
> what would you say, except that he has sown
> troubles for himself and much laughter for his enemies?
> 　(641–47)

We find several interesting features here: men, explicitly, pray for obedient offspring, but implicit in Creon's formulation is the idea that children will obey their fathers. The only real question is whether these children will honor the father's *philoi* as much as they do the father (643–44). Even more interesting, however, are the last two lines quoted above, because they remind us of Hesiod's *Works and Days*:

> Marry a young woman, so that you can teach her good
> 　manners,
> [and especially marry one who lives near to you,]
> looking at everything, all around, lest you marry a source
> 　of joy for the neighbors.
> for a man carries off nothing better than a good wife,
> nor anything more painful than an evil one. (699–703)

Sophocles has taken the potential instability of a wife who, if bad, will amuse the neighbors, and has transferred it to the offspring. The move is not unlikely, since indeed a bad wife might be expected to produce bad, or even illegitimate, children. Creon's speech, however, rewrites the danger of marriage as a danger to the relationship of father and son. Unlike Hesiod, who advises merely to choose a "maiden" and try to control her, Creon bypasses the woman altogether, focusing his attention on controlling his (male) children.

Similarly, when it comes to the issue of whom Haemon will marry, Creon makes it clear that, in his eyes, the woman is the replaceable party in a marriage; for when Ismene asks him point blank, "But will you kill the bride of your own child?" he responds "[Yes], for the lands of others are plowable" (569). Creon's line would call to mind the Athenian wedding formula.[5] * * * But it also makes clear the construct that the formula implies: the woman in marriage is an object of exchange for the purpose of bearing children, and as such, she can be painlessly traded in without damage to the identity of the *oikos*.[6] Creon's views of Antigone may be in part politically

---

5. Spoken by the bride's father to the groom: "I entrust, I give her to you to have legitimate children by plowing."
6. Household.

motivated. But they also fit the stock views of women held by men in patrilineal, homosocial society.

Toward the end of Haemon's scene with his father, Creon emphasizes the importance of his direct bond with Haemon, and again tries to deny Antigone's sexual dominion over his son:

> HAE.: If you were not my father, I would have said you aren't thinking well.
> CR.: Since you are a woman's slave, don't fawn on me. (755–56)

The idea that Haemon is "enslaved" by his eros is again a stock characterization, but one that emphasizes through exaggeration the dangers of female sexuality. If Haemon is going to let that woman mediate between them, Creon seems to suggest, then their father–son relationship is in peril. Desperately, at the end of the exchange, Creon suggests that he will have Antigone killed in front of Haemon, the clearest possible attempt to create a bond with his son that excludes his son's fiancee. When we consider the tendency for women to be portrayed as sacrificial victims at the moment of their marriage (e.g., Iphigenia), we might even see this as an attempted sacrifice, one that will restore Creon's optimum order. It will remove Antigone, and in forcing Haemon to watch her death, it will implicate his approval—or at least his acceptance—of that death, in obedience to his father.

This view of the family contrasts sharply with the view put forth by Antigone, a view that she hints at from the first line of the play. Antigone begins, "Dear Ismene, my sister of the same parents." This might emphasize no more than her closeness to her sister. Segal,[7] however, has noticed a pattern of kinship words especially prevalent in Antigone's speech. At 466–67, she refers to Polyneices as "from my mother," and at 511 she argues, "For it is not at all shameful to honor those from the same *splanchna*." *Splanchna* means, literally, "womb." In short, Antigone "makes kinship a function of the female procreative power," and the first line of the play also fits into this category. Segal points out that *adelphos*[8] comes from *a-* ("same") and *delphys* ("womb"). At this point Antigone still seeks the help of her sister, and so includes her in the *maternal* line by which she defines the family. Later, when she has dismissed her sister as weak-hearted, she still sees the king's bloodline as going through herself (though only through herself). About to go to her death, Antigone invokes the chorus: "Look at the only remainder of the king's line" (940–41). Her definition of

---

7. Charles Segal, *Tragedy and Civilization: An Interpretation of Sophocles* (Cambridge, MA: Harvard UP, 1981), 183–86.
8. Of a sibling.

the family, both hers and her parents', grants specific powers of kinship to the female. Creon's idealized father–son lineage, then, directly opposes Antigone's implicit recognition of female mediation and participation.

Creon, therefore, defines the family differently than does Antigone. In his talk with Haemon, he tries to create a male homosocial line similar to that established by Heracles at the end of the *Trachiniae*. As several commentators have pointed out, however, Creon's political power is all too dependent on the maternal lineage that Antigone implies. He states, in his first speech, "I hold all the power and the throne / through my close relationship [*anchisteia*] to the dead" (173–74). *Anchisteia* is, of course, a specific legal term defining the order of inheritance within a family. Though we cannot assume that Creon is bound by fifth-century Athenian law, he bases his power on a familial relationship and uses terminology that would certainly recall inheritance disputes for the audience. What that terminology does not state, but must be understood to mean, is that Creon's right to the throne comes to him through his sister, Jocasta. He has no patrilineal relation to the two dead brothers.

The importance of Creon's *anchisteia* becomes even more clear when we hit a wickedly funny pun about twenty lines later. Creon here makes the public proclamation to which Antigone had referred at the beginning of the play: "And now, having announced these things I hold their brother-announcements, / for the citizens concerning the children of Oedipus" (192–93). Notice that for Creon, the two dead warriors are sons of Oedipus, not of Jocasta. His decree, however, is "from the same womb" (*a-delphos*) as the things he has just been saying. Many will not agree that the word *adelphos* calls to mind the idea of a womb. In the light of the familial definitions that appear in this passage, and in the light of Antigone's appeal in the first line to her *autadelphos* sister, however, I take *adelphos* as meaning (at least) "brother to" these principles. To understand the word as such is to recall the relationship that Creon specifically refuses to acknowledge in his decree: the relationship of Polyneices and Eteocles as brothers, whom Antigone will address as "from the same womb." Creon's proclamation, like his power, is matrilineal, however much he might like to overlook that fact. He cannot exclude female mediation.

JUDITH FLETCHER

Sophocles' *Antigone* and the Democratic Voice[†]

The citizens of fifth-century B.C.E. Athens who wrote, produced, performed, watched, and judged Greek tragedy accepted certain
anachronisms in the depiction of a mythological past that focused
on the catastrophic lives of a few royal families. Among the most
striking is how democratic law-making processes familiar to the
Athenian audience (and a relatively recent political system) are projected onto the monarchies of myth and legend. In Aeschylus' *Suppliant Women*, King Pelasgus, responding to the Danaids' petition
for sanctuary, insists on seeking the approval of the assembly of
Argive citizens, whose voting practices are pointedly emphasized in
the text (*Supp.* 607). Theseus, that archetype of democratic principles, refers to the judicial processes of Athens in Sophocles' *Oedipus at Colonus* (1051–3), and consults the Athenian populace when
he decides to champion the cause of Argive mothers in Euripides'
Suppliant Women (404–8). Less benign (but perhaps more democratic) is the Argive assembly who vote to stone their prince Orestes
for matricide (Euripides' *Orestes* 440–2), or the Greek army at Troy,
whose motion to sacrifice the captive Trojan princess Polyxena,
reproduces the enactment formula that preceded the decrees passed
by the Athenian democratic assembly of the fifth century (Euripides'
Hecuba 107–8).

When tragedy mirrors the legislative processes of Athenian democracy, it makes the heroic world of mythology more familiar and
accessible to the fifth-century citizen audience, but it is important
to note that the legal practices of Athens are not embedded in its
drama in any simplistic or merely self-congratulatory manner.
Law is represented as a complicated and sometimes precarious
power. Tragedy gives careful consideration to how the language of
law can create the social world: the decrees engendered by the legislative bodies represented in drama are all examples of what philosophers of language such as J. L. Austin and John Searle have
identified as speech acts or illocutions. In classical Athens, some of
the most authoritative speech acts were collectively voiced by citizens in the legislative assembly and law courts. Their edicts and

† From *Interrogating Antigone in Postmodern Philosophy and Criticism*, ed. S. E. Wilmer
and Audronė Žukauskaitė (Oxford: Oxford University Press, 2010), pp. 168–84. Reprinted
with permission of *Mosaic Journal*. An earlier version of this article originally appeared as
"Citing the Law in Sophocles's *Antigone*" in *Mosaic, an interdisciplinary critical journal*
41.3 (2008): 79–96. Unless otherwise indicated, notes are by the author. Some of the
author's notes have been omitted.

decrees exemplify Sandy Petrey's synthesis of the performative utterance as 'a combination of language and social practice', which functions 'within the conventional interactions that characterize a given sociohistorical group.[1]

The homologies of Athenian law and its theatre have often been noted—their shared audience and actors, their rule-governed scripts. Like a dramatic text, a law or decree is programmatic; it prescribes what people say or do. A legal speech act, such as a decree, functions in tragedy as a potent generator of plot and action. To use Austin's terminology, the tragic events that emanate from an edict (for example, the sacrifice of Polyxena) are the perlocutions of the speech act. Oedipus' decree condemning the murderer of Laius (*Oedipus Tyrannos* 223–51) replicates Athenian legal procedure for investigating and prosecuting a homicide. It sets in motion a series of perlocutionary consequences that cause the edict to recoil on its author, who turns out to be that murderer. Tragedy, it would seem, not only echoes the performative language of law, but exposes its fallibilities as well. In this respect, Sophocles' *Antigone* holds a special place in any consideration of the representation of law in tragedy, since it poses fundamental and disturbing questions about the capacity of language to create law, the relationship between law and force, and specifically, as this chapter will argue, about the role of the citizenry in law-making.

I do not intend to argue that this tragedy represents any specific political situation in fifth-century Thebes or Athens, although as Richard Seaford notes, Sophocles' Theban plays might have reassured Athens that the 'horrors of tyranny are projected onto the mythical past . . . [and] are safely projected onto Thebes'. The Thebes of tragedy may be the 'Anti-Athens', as Froma Zeitlin put it,[2] but I maintain that there is a democratic voice embedded in this text which suggests that the civic ideology of Athens is a natural and unquenchable force. Christiane Sourvinou-Inwood is justifiably cautious about reading Sophocles' Thebes as a 'mimetic representation of Athenian democracy', but she does advocate a reception of the play that takes into account the cultural and political context of its production, that is, democratic Athens.[3] Her conception of how this reception operated and its relationship to democracy is substantially different from mine, however. My approach to the play is one that takes into account its status as a cultural product of 'a festival of the democratic polis', that is informed by and sustains an ideology generated by a system in which the democratic collective 'ruled through its control of public speech'.[4]

1. Petrey (1990: 13).
2. Seaford (2000: 42–3); Zeitlin (1990: 130–67).
3. Sourvinou-Inwood (1989: 134–48).
4. Ober (1993: 483).

The project of this chapter then is to consider how such democratic forces manifest themselves in this fictional version of Thebes. My strategy will be to examine the trajectory of Creon's interdiction forbidding the burial of Polyneices from its inception to its reception and eventual annulment. This command helps us to frame an important question about language and law: what gives a legal performative its status beyond its utterance by a powerful civic figure? By considering the interdiction as a speech act that becomes part of public discourse and is disseminated through the various channels of communication in the polis, I hope to expose the infelicities and distortions which vitiate its status as law. Unlike the 'democratic' monarchs of tragedy, Theseus or Pelasgus, Creon does not consult the citizens of Thebes before he makes his announcement forbidding the burial. We might assume that he composed this prohibition on the battlefield where there would be no opportunity for deliberation, but he does announce it a second time to the assembly of Theban Elders without any debate or consultation. It is my contention, nonetheless, that the voice of the *dêmos* (the citizens) is by no means silent in this text, which reflects some of the informal discursive structures of Athenian democracy.

First, however, we need to determine if there is any chance that the fifth-century audience could conceive of Creon's interdiction as a law. Creon refers to his proclamation as a *nomos*, a slippery term which can mean 'established custom', or 'law'. Antigone describes the burial of Eteocles and the defenders of Thebes as being the 'right use of custom (*tôi nomôi*, 24)'; she explicitly denies that Creon's interdiction is a law. How would the original audience of this tragedy view her denial and challenge? In her influential article, Sourvinou-Inwood argues that we need to set aside our contemporary focus on individual freedoms which make us hostile to Creon's position. Creon represents the polis, and in every Greek city-state of the fifth century, it was the polis that authorized religious activities, including funeral rituals. Antigone is overstepping her limitations by claiming to know what the gods want; only Teiresias has the authority to do this. The fact that Teiresias substantiates Antigone's claims should not, according to Sourvinou-Inwood, affect our reading of the play, since we need to put ourselves in the position of the audience who cannot read ahead. Because the ruling power of Thebes has issued the prohibition, it was necessary for all Thebans to obey, regardless of their private feelings. The prohibition (*kêrugma*) on burying Polyneices seems to echo an Athenian law forbidding the burial of traitors within the city walls. Generals sometimes pronounced *kêrugmata* on the battlefield, and it was the duty of the common citizen to comply.

Larry Bennett and William Blake Tyrrell offer a different perspective: 'Antigone acts correctly because she does not defy Creon, leader of Athens, but Creon, the totalitarian ruler of impious Thebes'.[5] Edward Harris implicitly supports this approach by analysing what the ingredients of law were to an Athenian audience, and how Creon fails to create a true law. I shall return to some of his arguments later in this chapter, but the germane point for now is that Athenian citizens swore the Ephebic Oath, promising to 'obey those who are ruling prudently and the established laws and those which they may prudently establish for themselves in the future'. In other words, blind obedience to the commands of a ruling power was not an obligation if those commands were not sensible. Indeed, epic poetry and tragedy is consistent in how it recognizes the need for proper burial. While an Athenian law might have prevented burying traitors in Attica, it did not prevent traitors from being taken outside Attic borders for burial. Proper burial of the dead is a fundamental concern of the Greeks. The Homeric gods are disturbed by the defilement of Hector's corpse in *Iliad* 24. Sophocles' *Ajax* and Euripides' *Suppliant Women* both deal with the crisis of unburied corpses. Indeed, Creon himself, after hearing the prediction of Teiresias, decides to bury the corpse because 'it is best to obey established laws' (1113–14).

Certainly, by the end of the *Antigone* it becomes obvious that the gods were offended by Creon's interdiction, but would an Athenian audience have to wait for the prophecy of Teiresias before they recognized not only the impiety of the prohibition, but also its innate illegality? It is my contention that the dramatic architecture of Sophocles' *Antigone* suggests the instability of the interdiction and its illusory status as law from the opening lines of the prologue. Antigone will never call this interdiction a 'law' (*nomos*), but only a *kêrugma* ('announcement'), a word cognate with *kêrux*, 'herald', and she will never call Creon king, but merely *strategos*, general, that is, a type of magistrate. Her position toward Creon's interdiction is that of an Athenian citizen who had the right to denounce a magistrate for malfeasance and who recognizes and demonstrates that the authority of law resides in a power that transcends Creon's articulation of a command.

It is thus significant that the first person to speak in the play is not Creon announcing the edict, but Antigone complaining about it to Ismene. The play opens at an important moment in the communication of the prohibition: its reception by the very person who will contravene and obstruct it: 'And what is this announcement (*kêrugma*) that they say the general (*strategos*) has just now made for the entire city?' (7–8). Antigone answers her own question by quoting the *kêrugma* transmitted to her by a process of public

5. Tyrrell and Bennett (1998: 42).

communication. On first consideration, the *kêrugma* seems to fulfil the criteria required of a felicitous speech act identified by Austin (34): an 'appropriate figure', the most powerful man of Thebes, possessing 'the appropriate authority', has issued a command in the 'appropriate circumstances', a public forum (presumably the battlefield before the play began). But as events unfold, it seems that Creon's *kêrugma* has a rather subversive energy that radiates beyond its initial utterance; its status as a citation—necessary for it to take effect—somehow undermines its authority. In other words, Creon can make his pronouncement, but he cannot control the context of its reception and repetition.

When Antigone repeats the interdiction to her sister, she highlights its transmission; *kêrux* words are significant in this speech, which lays stress on the announcement of the proclamation, and a reference to the process of its transmission.

> Eteocles, *so they say*, thinking it just to make right use of custom, he has buried in the earth, to be honored by the dead beneath. But the wretchedly dead corpse of Polyneices it has been announced (*ekkekêruchthai*) to all the citizens, *they say*, that no man may cover with a grave nor lament. That is what, *they say*, noble Creon has proclaimed (*kêrukschant' echein*) for you and me, for me I tell you. (*Ant.* 22–32)

Antigone's citational practices ('they say', 'it has been announced', etc.) emphasize that the utterance has been removed from its author, a necessary function of its status as a civic announcement. It is not only Creon's articulation of the interdiction that gives it legs, but also its repetition by a public voice. An audience who participated in the making of law would be aware that the *kêrugma* is circulated by the citizens of Thebes who made no contribution to its formulation. Although in his opening speech Creon claims to value the counsel of his subjects (179), he later reveals his tyrannical nature by insisting to Haemon that the city belongs to its ruler (738). With complete incredulity, he asks his son if it is the polis who will tell *him* what he must order (734). Creon's unilateral edict is a strong contrast to the many ancient sources which describe law as a product of common consent: Demosthenes (25.16), for example, asserts that law is 'a general agreement of the entire community'. As we have already noted, Athenian tragedy regularly espouses the requirement for communal participation in the legislative process, even in states ruled by mythical kings. Tragedy might be set in a mythical past, and feature legendary monarchies, but the most reasonable sovereigns seem to adhere to democratic principles. There is no evidence, however, that the citizens of Thebes make any contribution to the interdiction other than to circulate Creon's decree.

Is there any indication that Creon has the support of the citizens, whose city he purportedly wishes to enhance (191)? Charles Segal describes the interdiction as 'public speech' represented in the opening scene as 'part of an anonymous, ill-defined public voice'.[6] He understands the public voice and Creon's broadcast of the decree to be unanimous. But is it? It is true that the Chorus offers no objections; Ismene apparently assumes that since the people of Thebes transmit the decree they must approve of it; she feels helpless to act 'in defiance of the city' (79). Even Antigone eventually submits to the idea that she is acting 'against the will of the city' (907). She can hardly be blamed for feeling abandoned as she is led to her death and taunted by the Chorus of Theban Elders (509), although earlier she had suggested to Creon that the Chorus agreed with her position even if they were afraid to speak out in his presence. More importantly, there are strong indications that the Chorus of Yes-men are not representative of public opinion, that Creon is not the singular voice of Thebes, and that behind his back a dissident group of voices whisper their disapproval.

Creon himself is well aware of malcontents who 'from the very start muttered secretly against me' (290–1). He mistakenly believes that dissenters have bribed the guards so they can bury the corpse, but nonetheless he is aware that people are talking about his order behind his back. In defence of Antigone, Haemon corroborates Creon's realization of community unrest with an eloquent account of the disapproval of the *dêmos* (683–723). He tells his father that the population of Thebes denies that Antigone is wrong to bury her brother; this would surely include the people who transmitted Creon's interdiction to Antigone. This may not be a government where the *dêmos* contributes to the making of law with a vote, but the public voice does comment on Creon's autocratic proclamation. Antigone's citation of the *dêmos* in her quotation of the *kêrugma* is neutral, but Haemon is especially insistent on the voices of the community who commend Antigone's action and condemn the edict. Haemon can overhear what the city is saying 'in the shadows' (692–3) and how it mourns Antigone, who dies undeservedly for a praiseworthy act. This report of what the city says includes a version of his father's interdiction that dogs and birds will prey on the corpse (cf. 205–6), an illustration of how the pronouncement is quoted and critiqued by the citizens of Thebes. The public announcement of Creon thus becomes a 'dark secretive report' that spreads throughout the city (700). These irrepressible but anonymous voices are a powerful

6. Segal (1981: 161).

reminder that Creon does not have total command of the discourse in every context of the polis, despite his fantasy of absolute control. Although the Chorus of Elders may be afraid to oppose him openly, the polis includes a background of citizen voices, citing and critiquing the command—voices which have circulated its contents so effectively that Antigone can repeat them, and Haemon can report the permutations of his father's edict.

So it seems that underneath the official position we can detect a clamour of informal debates and disagreements. The text features an assortment of voices, some sympathetic towards Antigone's position, others less so, and this polyphony, a chief factor in the undeniably slippery quality of the tragedy, helps to represent the manifold voices which constitute a polis, even an autocratic polis. The play was written for an audience whose understanding of law-making included a democratic debate. The *ekklêsia* (the democratic assembly) where laws were created was a raucous uproar of competing opinions: the trained speakers who bantered back and forth, and also the common men, the *dêmos*, whose collective disapproval or approbation was expressed by their vote, but also less formally as a clamour, a *thorubus*, that arose in the assembly and was 'a crucial element of Athenian democracy . . . in which ordinary people could make their thoughts known'.[7] Thucydides, Plato, and others report this *thorubus*, catcalls, boos, cheers, and shouting, not only in the assembly, but also in the courts where laws were enacted. The clamour of the *corona*, the bystanders, and their *thorubos* of dissent or approval provided one of the unofficial, but necessary, checks on the juries. I suggest then that the dissent that Haemon reports to his father should be understood as just such a *thorubus* of dissapproval.

The 'dark secret report' is also a form of gossip, another important form of unofficial communication in Athens. Antigone and Ismene depend on gossip and rumour for Creon's message, since they were obviously not present at the initial utterance of the proclamation. Yet Creon himself does not hear what is said in the back alleys and dark corners of his realm; he sends, but he does not receive. Gossip was a powerful means of transmitting information back and forth between the public and private spheres in the Athenian democracy; it contributed to a two-way stream of communication lacking in Thebes. Contrastingly, the Athenian political system allowed for the flow of rumour back into more formal modes of discourse. Josiah Ober lists gossip and rumour as one of several political forums of debate and communication, along with the courts, assembly, and theatre, where Athenian citizens could

7. Tacon (2001: 180).

exchange information and ideas with each other.[8] Speakers in law courts exploited the conception of Athens as a face-to-face community in which everyone knew everyone else's business, either by frequenting the *agora* (town square/market-place), or shops, or through prostitutes and entertainers at drinking parties. Plutarch (*Nicias* 30.1) records how news of the devastating naval disaster at Sicily in 416 B.C.E. was first heard in a barber shop, and travelled rapidly throughout the city. Rumour was an important means of disseminating information and sharing opinions between the common citizen and the elite members of society. Furthermore, as Virginia Hunter has shown, gossip could be integral to the public scrutiny of magistrates, the *dokimasia*, when it would be woven into Athenian political discourse in a useful manner.

Thebes is abuzz with talk of the interdiction and Antigone's defiance, but the informal yet conventional modes of communication (the *thorubos* and gossip) which had authority in the Athenian democracy, are occluded in the Theban tyranny. The Guard's reluctance to report the burial to Creon suggests a cowed populace afraid to bring unwelcome news to their king. But Antigone seems to have activated a shadow *dêmos*, a ghostly whisper of the uncontainable *vox populi* and its *thorubos*. Public talk has become displaced in Thebes—squeezed into private conversations and secret debates—but it cannot be completely silenced. From the first moments of the play, Antigone appears to have taken control of the discourse and to become a vital part of the reception and transmission of democratic talk. This in itself is perhaps one of the most striking examples of the discursive disturbances of Thebes. As Thucydides makes Pericles say, the ideal woman is 'the least mentioned' (2.45.2); the absence of any female voice from fifth-century Athens suggests the advice was heeded. Not only is Antigone mentioned quite a bit in Thebes, but she speaks out in a political context. Creon's effects on the channels of civic discourse apparently include the erosion of the ideal of decorous feminine silence. Antigone is thus both a symptom of and a remedy for Thebes' distorted discursive system.

Antigone's intrusion into public talk is evident in the prologue: she first cites Creon's *kêrugma*, precisely where Creon will publish it himself, on the steps of the royal residence, but then she also performs her own speech act in this same spot: 'I myself will bury him,' she declares to her sister, 'I will lie dead beside him' (71–3). Ismene, paradigm of feminine docility, timidly recommends silence about the plan, but Antigone insists upon public broadcast of her speech act: 'Oh no! Announce it. You should be much more hateful, if you keep quiet and not proclaim (*kêrukses*) this to everyone' (86–7).

8. Ober (1983: 148–51).

The prologue, which opened by emphasizing how public information had seeped into an intimate moment between two sisters, draws
to a close as Antigone begins her intervention into public discourse.
She expropriates the vocabulary of Creon's order for her own act of
defiance: she wants the burial of her brother to be announced
(*kêrukses*) in the same way that Creon's ban was announced. As
Judith Butler notes, 'Like Creon . . . Antigone wants her speech act
to be radically and comprehensively public'; and for Segal, 'Usurping his word, she mounts a total challenge to the civic *logos*'.[9]

Given the impropriety of female speech in the public sphere,
Antigone's role as the voice of democratic law might seem anomalous.
It is true that women of citizen status in Athens did not speak out
in public, much less participate in debates about law, but Antigone's
social identity as a virgin gives her special symbolic status for several reasons. The Athenian audience of this play worshipped Athena,
a virgin goddess, who dispensed laws. More generally, *Dikê* (Justice)
is traditionally personified as a virgin. Hesiod describes the murmur
of protest that spreads among the people when the virgin *Dikê* is
dragged off by evil men (*Works and Days* 220–1), a passage that suggests the *thorubos* of disapproval by the Theban citizens in Sophocles' play. Likewise, the allegorical figure *Demokratia* is a young
woman. Furthermore, the orators of the fourth century exploited the
mythology of sacrificial virgins as a model for young male citizens
who were being incorporated into the polis; the daughters of the
Athenian King Erectheus, who willingly sacrificed themselves on
behalf of the state, were used by the fourth-century orators as a paradigm of courage for Athenian youths.

All things considered then, it is somewhat anti-climactic when
Creon makes *his* announcement (for the second time) to his council
of Elders. Concurrently, Antigone, whose citation and usurpation of
the *kêrugma* have been given priority of placement, is defying the
interdiction even as it is spoken—a dramatic contrast to the com-
pliant Chorus. The Elders, having been summoned to hear the
kêrugma, account for their presence in this public space: they have
been called for a *sunklêton leschên*, a 'convened assembly,' by a 'public announcement' (*koinôi kêrugmati*) (160–1), terminology that
evokes the summoning of the democratic assembly in Athens. But
they offer no argument or comment; all they can say in response is
'if it is pleasing to you' (211), an ironic contrast to the enactment
formula, 'it seems best to the people', that preceded Athenian
decrees. Creon's announcement is delivered in an official-sounding
formal register: 'I have proclaimed (*kêruksas*) to the citizens', 192;
'it has been proclaimed' (*ekkêkeruktai*, 203). Again *kêrux* words

9. Butler (2000: 28); Segal (1981: 62).

predominate, but this vocabulary is far removed from the language of Athenian law-making. This is a command fashioned for a very specific circumstance, yet it is in the nature of law to apply to general situations. Aristotle's comment that every law is 'about a general matter' (*Politics* 1137b11–14, 27–9) is illustrated by the phrasing of Athenian laws for example, 'If anyone destroys the democracy at Athens . . .' (Andocides 1.96).

The subsequent confrontation between Antigone and Creon would have a special resonance for the Athenian audience of the play. The process of creating laws and decrees in their political structure embraced the important principle of *isêgoria*, the right of every citizen to debate in the assembly. It is quite obviously a freedom that does not exist in Creon's regime, but Antigone enacts the role of the citizen who had the right to disagree and debate about any motion made in the assembly. Hannah Roisman appropriately hears her as the voice of free speech. Unlike the Watchman, the Chorus, or the cowed Theban polity, Antigone speaks without fear in the presence of Creon. When Creon tells her that his proclamation is a law (*nomous*, 449), she fearlessly disputes him. As I have argued, the structure and subtext of the drama emphasize the infelicities of Creon's interdiction. In her much-admired argument, Antigone is able to articulate related deficiencies when she makes the distinction between one man's proclamation and true *nomos*:

> As far as I'm concerned, Zeus did not make this proclamation
>   (*kêruksas*)
> nor did Justice, who dwells with the gods below, enact such
>   laws (*nomous*)
> for mortals. And I don't think that your announcements
>   (*kêrugmata*)
> are so strong that they enable a mortal to outrun the unwritten and
> unshakeable (*asphalê*) laws (*nomima*) of the gods. (450–5)

The passage emphasizes the deficiencies of Creon's proclamation in several ways: first and foremost, his *kêrugma* is not sanctioned by the gods, which is to say Creon does not possess 'the appropriate authority' to make it. A popular analysis interprets the play as a conflict between civic law and divine law, but this concept is not natural to Greek thought; the Greeks understood true law to come from the gods. According to tradition, legendary law-makers such as Solon received laws directly from a deity. It is the goddess Athena who bestows a court of law on her city at the end of Aeschylus' *Eumenides*. As the philosopher Heraclitus put it, 'the laws of men are nourished by one law, the divine law' (fr. 253 Kirk-Raven; 114 Deils-Kranz). Demosthenes (25.16) likewise states that 'every law is an invention and gift of the gods'. Sophocles himself describes law as coming from Zeus (*OT* 863–70). If the just laws of the polis are intrinsically divine, then obviously Creon's interdiction cannot be a law.

Antigone's second point is to compare the instability of Creon's order with the laws of the gods, which are unwritten. The notion of 'unwritten laws' is not unique to this text, but recurs in other contemporary sources. They are, in the words of Rosalind Thomas, 'a preexisting set of customs, traditions and assumptions onto which written laws were grafted'.[1] They existed before law codes were written down, and included the treatment of one's parents, the worship of the gods, and proper treatment of the dead. While they are not specific to one polis, and common to a diversity of peoples, they are not normally set in opposition to the laws of the state. Greek thought tends to represent the two forms of *nomos* as complementing one another. In Thebes, however, an interdiction against burying the dead cannot be grafted onto or supported by the laws of the gods; it contradicts divine *nomos*, and so is not really a law.

Antigone's dichotomy between the unwritten laws of the gods and Creon's order poses an interesting problem. If the laws of the gods are unwritten, does this align the *kêrugma* with writing? And if it does, how does this quality bear upon the transmission of the interdiction through the medium of public repetition? Antigone does not say that the *kêrugma* is written, but in a sense it is. Writing suggests the possibility of repetition, what Jacques Derrida calls 'iterability', precisely the feature of the *kêrugma* that results in its dissemination. Writing also allows for a separation between author and utterance, a phenomenon exemplified by the various repetitions of Creon's interdiction throughout the city. The ancient audience could understand that an order like Creon's, which has not been grafted onto the fixed universal laws, could be erased and 'rewritten', unlike the permanence of divine *nomima*.

Another indication of its lack of stability is the emendable quality of the *kêrugma*. Like a written document, it can be erased and rewritten, a quality suggested by its apparently unstable penalty. Antigone claims that the penalty for disobedience is public stoning (36), but in his proclamation to the Chorus, Creon specifies no penalty. Once her transgression has been revealed, he sets the punishment of entombment for Antigone to avoid polluting the city with her death (773–80), a rather curious concession from a man willing to leave a corpse to rot in the sun. Explanations of this apparent deviation are various: that Antigone adds a bit of her own 'emotional embroidery' with the detail, or that Creon has been partly

1. Thomas (2005: 54).

affected by Haemon's arguments. Whatever reconstruction we imagine, the conclusion has to be that Creon's word is not stable, or to use Antigone's term, *asphalê*, if it can be subjected to modifications or amendments.

At this point, it should be apparent that Creon's order, his *kêrugma*, exists throughout the play as an impermanent creation, always, it seems, in flux, and never completely within Creon's control. Its illocutionary authority is explicitly denied by Antigone who refuses to abide by it and so dies. But this does not confirm the force of Creon's words, since the circumstances of her death underscore the limitations of his linguistic authority. She made her own declaration in the prologue: 'I will lie dead beside him' (73). She conspicuously disobeys the edict, and insults its author, forcing him to enforce it. As Nicole Loraux remarks, Antigone 'chose to die by her own will and so to change execution into suicide'.[2] Her suicide draws attention to the king's inability to control the effects of language, since it occurs after Creon has ordered Antigone to be saved. There is a tragic symmetry, characteristically Sophoclean, in this organization: as Creon makes the command, Antigone defies it; as Creon says that he will rescue Antigone, she kills herself.

Thus, on his first day as king, Creon discovers that language is not so much a blunt instrument as it is an uncontainable fluid. The tyrant is slow to learn that he cannot control the city with his words. He absolutely refuses to authorize any other voice until Teiresias speaks. The blind prophet delivers two warnings to Creon, the first based on his reading of the bird signs, a signifying system that has become distorted by their feast of human meat. The process itself is a form of reading: the boy attendant describes the bird signs and sacrifices, Teiresias interprets and cites the text, as it were, to Creon. Yet as long as his initial attempts to move Creon are structured as a chain of citations, he remains ineffective. It will not be the signs cited by Teiresias that persuade Creon, but a more direct communiqué. An important shift occurs when Teiresias changes register in his second *rhesis* (1064–90); now speaking in a powerful mantic voice that motivates Creon's change of heart, he utters a forceful prophecy of disaster described as *akinêta*, 'unmoveable' (1060). 'You provoke me to speak the immoveable secrets (*akinêta*) of my soul', he groans after Creon has uttered his most blasphemous rebuttal. The term *akinêta* conveys the violent exposure of some securely lodged truth; it could be accurately translated as 'steadfast' or 'secure', in other words as a synonym for *asphalê*. Teiresias apparently speaks from the same place, has access to the same divine truths, as Antigone. She spoke in reference to steadfast (*asphalê*)

2. Loraux (1987: 31–2).

laws authored by the gods which should manifest as universal moral laws or precepts. Teiresias refers to a divinely authored consequence of breaking these laws, a consequence which he would prefer to keep hidden and so *akinêta*. But the deeper implications of his *akinêta* are that they come directly from the gods; this prophecy is not obtained by interpreting the boy's description of the sacrifice, but rather through an immediate intuitive process that involves no reading of symbols—in this respect, they also qualify as *agrapta*, unwritten. There is no separation between author and reader in his case, but a mystical process by which he acquires unmediated knowledge. Teiresias' revelations validate Antigone's insistence that her brother must be buried, and validate this conviction with terminology that recalls her own arguments.

Since Teiresias has direct access to the divine, he adds weight to Antigone's contention that Creon's announcement is not what he says it is—a law. A mortal cannot make a command that supersedes the authority of the gods. But Creon's utterance is performative; it does set a series of tragic events in motion, although these consequences are not the ones he intended. If the utterance is not a law, then what is it? One of Searle's modifications to Austin's inaugural theory was to make a distinction between speech acts that are ratified by communal protocols (this would include making laws) and individual speech acts such as promises, wagers, threats, and insults, which turn on social protocol but do not necessarily require an explicit formula or authorization. Creon's interdiction pretends to fit into the former category—an institutional speech act or law— but in fact falls into the latter, a threat by an individual. Creon does things with words, since various members of the community are intimidated by his threat (the Watchman, for example, guards the corpse and apprehends Antigone). But like his predecessor Oedipus, who issued a decree that turned out to have more impact on its author than any other citizen in Thebes, Creon makes a proclamation that has devastating personal consequences for himself—the loss of his son and then his wife; in essence, the eradication of his family line.

Antigone (whose name means 'against the family') has turned out to be a powerful agent of his catastrophe, and concomitantly the agent who reveals the flaws in his attempt to make law. She too has made a speech act; Timothy Gould aptly calls this a play about 'a conflict of performatives'.[3] Her announcement—which appears to be an individual promise—turns out to have the institutional force that Creon's illocution lacks. But she too has her limitations. Antigone herself was not able to persuade Creon that the unburied corpse of

3. Gould (1995: 41).

her brother offended the gods. This is an important point conso-
nant with a society and a genre that associated authoritative speech
with men. The original dramatic production might have emphasized the disparity by having the same actor play both Antigone and
Teiresias: only when the actor portrays a male character does his
voice have authority for Creon. It is not until Teiresias confirms
that the laws of the gods have been violated that Antigone's similar
assertion is authenticated. Teiresias predicts that within a few days
Creon will repay corpse for corpses 'because you keep up here one
who belongs to the gods below, a corpse unburied, unhonored,
all unhallowed' (1070–1, Jebb's translation). Apparently, then,
Antigone's burial of her brother was not a complete act. As J. E. G.
Whitehorne notices, Antigone intended to perform the entire
multi-staged ceremony herself, first approaching Ismene for help
in lifting the body, and then planning to erect a monument over
the corpse. For the original audience of this play, a complete funeral
was a multi-staged event, with distinct activities for both genders:
women's roles consisted of pouring libations and mourning (as
described by the Watchman at 431), but responsibility for burying
the dead lay with the male members of a family. It is clear from
Teiresias' words that Antigone's attempt to take over this function
is innately defective; the gods clearly demand a more public, complete ritual.

Creon and Haemon are the only living male relatives who can
assume this role. In taking over the responsibility for her brother's
burial, Antigone had challenged Creon's position as the head of her
household, and 'as king of Thebes, the legal successor to the political
estate of Eteocles and Polyneices, its co-rulers'.[4] Helene Foley has
argued that Creon's refusal to bury Polyneices means that Antigone becomes an 'honorary male'; as she reminds us, the citizens
of Thebes had praised her for taking on this duty, an indication
that there were exceptional circumstances in which a woman might
act autonomously.[5] Appealing as this interpretation may be, it still
does not explain why Teiresias refers to the corpse as unburied, nor
does it account for the fact that Antigone cannot perform the ritual
as completely as she says she will. Sourvinou-Inwood is correct to
stress the need for ritual closure to satisfy the gods of the underworld. This is accomplished (too late) when Creon sets about performing the necessary rites. The messenger later describes the ritual
washing and arrangement of the corpse, the cremation, and the
raising of the monument (1199–1204), all performed by Creon.

4. Whitehorne (1983: 137).
5. Foley (2001: 180).

This would be a suitable point to return to Austin, who states that in order for a performative utterance to be effective 'the particular persons and circumstances in a given case must be appropriate for the invocation for the particular procedures invoked'. A saint, to use one of Austin's examples,[6] cannot baptize a penguin, and a woman, from the cultural perspective of an Athenian audience, cannot properly say, 'I will bury him'. She lacks the authority to make this particular promise since she is not the appropriate person to do so.

On the other hand, Antigone's insistence on inserting herself into public channels of communication and of speaking out in public functions as a necessary check on the abuse of language that Creon has perpetrated. Her performative utterance had the perlocutionary effect of her brother's official burial. Her speech act takes a most oblique route and possesses a strange spectral power, but her vow to bury her brother interfered with Creon's prohibition. By defying the edict, she sets in motion a chain of events that lead to Haemon's suicide; it is Teiresias' prophecy of this disaster that motivates Creon to bury Polyneices, foolishly believing that he has the power to change the gods' decrees, which unlike his own, cannot be erased. Creon performs the burial first in an attempt to deflect the gods' anger, but there are no second chances in this tragic universe. Harris is mistaken when he speculates that had she waited but a few hours, Creon would have rescued her and reunited her with Haemon. The prophecy of Teiresias allowed for no such conditions or alternatives; it was a speech act of unimpeachable authority.

Just as Antigone insinuated herself into an authorial position by speaking Creon's edict and then enacting its penalty on herself, so too her deformed speech act ('I will bury him') exposes Creon's considerable failures at language, his inability to say 'no-one will bury him'. The performative power of Antigone's words resides in an uncanny combination of quotations, and parodies, but she prevails. She operates in a shadow land of language which subtends the Theban autocracy where a tyrant's word is supposed to be law. Antigone's infelicities reveal her uncommon agency which is such that the pre-eminent male of Thebes, a King who should have the greatest authority to do things with words, cannot control his subjects by language. Moreover, he cannot even control the effects of his language. He ends up doing precisely that which he forbade. Creon attempts to create law unilaterally, ignoring both the voice of the *dêmos* and the laws of the gods. What develops is an aberration, a situation which forces a woman into the civic space, and requires her to speak on behalf of the *dêmos*. Antigone, whose action is the subject of muffled rumours and silent uproars, who creates a

6. Austin (1962: 15, 32–4).

98   JUDITH FLETCHER

scandal, becomes the embodiment of democratic debate, and the voice of true law.

Works Cited

Austin, J. L. *How to Do Things with Words*. Oxford: Oxford UP, 1962.
Butler, Judith. *Antigone's Claim: Kinship Between Life and Death*. New York: Columbia UP, 2000.
Foley, Helene. *Female Acts in Greek Tragedy*. Princeton: Princeton UP, 2001.
Gould, Timothy. "The Unhappy Performative." In *Performativity and Performance*, ed. Andrew Parker and Eve Kosovsky Sedgwick. New York: Routledge, 1995. 19–44.
Harris, Edward M. "Antigone the Lawyer, or the Ambiguities of *Nomos*." In *Law and the Courts in Ancient Greece*, ed. Edward M. Harris and Lene Rubinstein. London: Bloomsbury, 2004. 19–56.
Hunter, Virginia. "Gossip and Politics of Reputation in Classical Athens." *Phoenix* 44 (1990): 299–325.
Loraux, Nicole. *Tragic Ways of Killing a Woman*, trans. Anthony Foster. Cambridge, MA: Harvard UP, 1987.
Ober, Josiah. *Mass and Elite in Democratic Athens: Rhetoric, Ideology, and the Power of the People*. Princeton: Princeton UP, 1989.
Petrey, Sandy. *Speech Acts and Literary Theory*. New York: Routledge, 1990.
Roisman, Hanna M. "Women's Free Speech in Greek Tragedy." In *Free Speech in Classical Antiquity*, ed. Ineke Sluiter and Ralph M. Rosen. Leiden: Brill, 2004. 91–114.
Seaford, Richard. "The Social Function of Tragedy: A Response to Jasper Griffin." *Classical Quarterly* 50 (2000): 30–44.
Searle, John R. *Speech Acts: An Essay on the Philosophy of Language*. Cambridge: Cambridge UP, 1969.
Segal, Charles. *Tragedy and Civilization: An Interpretation of Sophocles*. Cambridge, MA: Harvard UP, 1981.
Sourvinou-Inwood, Christiane. "Assumptions and the Creation of Meaning: Reading Sophocles' *Antigone*." *Journal of Hellenic Studies* 109 (1989): 134–48.
Tacon, Judith. "Ecclesiastic *Thorubos*: Interventions, Interruptions, and Popular Involvement in the Athenian Assembly." *Greece & Rome* 48 (2001): 173–92.
Thomas, Rosalind. "Writer, Law and Written Law." In *The Cambridge Companion to Ancient Greek Law*, ed. Michael Gagarin and David Cohen. Cambridge: Cambridge UP, 2005. 41–60.
Tyrell, Wm. Blake, and Larry J. Bennett. "Sophocles' *Antigone* and Funeral Oratory." *American Journal of Philology* 111 (1990): 441–56.

Whitehorne, J. E. G. "The Background to Polyneices' Disinterment and Reburial." *Greece & Rome* 30 (1983): 129–42.
Zeitlin, Froma I. "Thebes: Theater of Self and Society in Athenian Drama." In *Greek Tragedy and Political Theory*, ed. J. Peter Euben. Berkeley: U of California P, 1990. 101–41. Reprinted in revised form in *Nothing to Do with Dionysos?: Athenian Drama in Its Social Context*, ed. John J. Winkler and Froma I. Zeitlin. Princeton: Princeton UP, 1990. 130–67.

CHARLES SEGAL

Lament and Closure in *Antigone*†

From antiquity to the present day the shrill voice of female lament in Greece has had an ambiguous relation to the rest of society. Women's lament helps the dead make the proper transition from the realm of the living to the other world but is also perceived as a source of emotional violence and disorder. It is associated with a maenadlike release of uncontrollable and disturbing emotions; and in its call for vengeance it can also lead to an unpredictable and uncontrollable cycle of vendettas, as one sees in Sophocles' *Electra* and in recent practices in some remote parts of modern Greece.

The control of this emotional energy was a continuing concern of ancient Greek society, and it is a recurrent subject of tragedy. Many cities kept female funerary rituals under some form of control or surveillance. In Athens, according to Plutarch, Solon established such laws to check the "disorderly and unbridled quality" of such lament, prohibiting breast-beating and wailing at funerals.[1] Tragedy exhibits two strategies of control: the transformation of the female voice into acceptable civic forms, and its suppression by masculine authority. The first is illustrated by the end of Aeschylus' *Oresteia*, in which Athena's persuasion transforms the Erinyes' curses into hymns of blessings (*Eumenides* 778–1047). On a smaller scale, Pindar's twelfth *Pythian Ode* tells how Athena, hearing the ululating wail of the two surviving Gorgons over their sister, Medusa, invents from it the flute-song known as the "many-headed tune" at Apollo's Pythian festival.

† From *Sophocles' Tragic World: Divinity, Nature, Society* (Cambridge, MA: Harvard University Press, 1998), pp. 119–23, 125–37. Copyright © 1995 by the President and Fellows of Harvard College. Used by permission. All rights reserved. Notes are by the editor of this Norton Critical Edition. The author's notes have been omitted.
1. Solon (630–530 B.C.E.): Athenian law giver. Plutarch (46–ca. 119 C.E.): ancient biographer.

The strategy of suppression (and its failure) is enacted in Sophocles' *Antigone*. Although the conflict in the play centers on the larger issue of prohibiting the burial of the traitorous brother Polyneices, it also involves the specific form of funerary lamentation; Antigone herself, caught in her defiant act of lamenting over her brother's body, is compared to a mother bird lamenting over its lost fledglings (422–428). The cry of a bird, often the nightingale, is an ancient figure for female lamentation and perhaps corresponds to a feeling that this intensely emotional utterance is akin to the wildness of nature and lies beyond familiar human discourse.

The ending of *Antigone* moves the scene of female funeral lament from the wild spaces outside the walls, where Antigone wails over Polyneices' corpse (422–431), to the house of Creon. The scene (1257–1353) is divided into two unequal parts, punctuated by the entrance of the Second Messenger with the news of Eurydice's suicide at 1278. The first section (1257–76) begins as a formal *thrēnos*, an antiphonal lament, which, however, is not between women, as it more commonly is in tragedy, but between men, the king and the elders of Thebes. The Theban elders announce Creon's arrival in terms that prepare for a scene of lamentation (1257–60): "And indeed here is our lord himself just come, bearing in his arms a conspicuous memorial [*mnēm' episēmon*], no other's disastrous folly [*atē*], if it is right to say it, but having himself erred." This formal lament by the authorities of the city creates the ritual closure familiar in so many Greek tragedies: the *Ajax, Hippolytus, Andromache, Oedipus at Colonus*, among others.

The term "conspicuous memorial" (*mnēm' episēmon*, 1258) refers specifically to the commemorative ceremonies of the public funeral and the entombment of warriors who have fallen in behalf of the city. In Pericles' Funeral Speech, about a decade later, those who have died fighting valorously for their country will have "a most conspicuous tomb" (*ton taphon episēmotaton*, Thucydides 2.43.2). This will consist of their fame in the living memory of the future, a memorial in the thoughts of men that does not need recording in writing (*agraphos mnēmē*, 2.43.3).

In such public rituals, the death of the individual is given continuity in the ongoing life of the community and its public functions. The ritual of burial that is begun with Creon's mourning over Haemon holds out a momentary hope that we might move toward a closure of this type. The movement toward a ritualizing closure in civic funerary ceremonies, however, is sharply interrupted by the shock of a new disorder, the suicide of Eurydice. Sophocles has artfully placed Creon's entrance with Haemon's body immediately after the long scene between Eurydice and the Messenger (1183–1256). The Messenger tells the sad tale of Haemon's death and then offers a hopeful interpretation of Eurydice's silent exit (1223–43). His optimism also looks toward the mood and context of a traditional funeral lament (1244–50):

> CHO. What conjecture would you make of this? The woman has gone straight back again before making an utterance, either good or bad.
>
> MESS. I myself stand in wonder, and yet I feed on hopes that hearing these woes of children she will not deem them worthy of lament in the city, but inside her house she will appoint her maidservants to cry out the private grief [*penthos oikeion*]. For she is not without good sense so as to fall into error.

But the scene ends with the Messenger's forebodings that the "heaviness of (Eurydice's) too great silence" holds some dread purpose that she "is hiding in secret, held down in her impassioned heart" (1253–56). This fear of some desperate act of female passion on the one side and her vehement laments and curses in her suicidal grief on the other (1301–05) frame Creon's lament over his son.

The contrast between the mourning ritual with which the chorus would enclose Haemon's death and Eurydice's way of mourning him reverses Creon's victory over Antigone in the first half of the play. In particular, the Theban elders of the chorus attempt to move their mourning away from the female lament, with its immersion in the pure grief of loss, toward a masculine and civic effacement of death's sorrow in civic "glory"; but the voice of maternal sorrow, like Antigone's voice earlier (423–427), proves the more powerful. Earlier in the play Creon has tried to assert the primacy of the city and its male rulers in matters dealing with death, but Antigone's desperate female mourning has challenged the claims of the city. When Creon again confronts the violent emotions of a mourning woman, he does so within his own house.

Creon has attempted to isolate the polis as a realm of autonomous, rational human control, but his assertion of an exclusively civic space breaks down when the prophet reveals the results of neglecting the rites of burial. Reading the signs of the gods' will in the cries and movements of the birds in the air and the flames around the slaughtered victims on the altars (998–1032), Teiresias demonstrates the link between the interior of the house and the cosmic space of sky and underworld. When Creon persists in his defiance, Teiresias displays the interconnectedness between the human community and the natural and supernatural worlds in a still more threatening form (1064–71):

> Know this well, that you shall not fulfill many racing courses of the sun before you shall give in exchange a corpse for corpses, one from your own loins, because you have hurled

below one of those above, placing her life in dishonored habi-
tation in a tomb, and because you keep here one who belongs
to the gods below, a corpse without his portion of honor,
without his rites of burial, without holiness.

Teiresias shoots this dread warning like a poisoned arrow into Creon's breast (1085–86; cf. 1033–34). His juxtapositions of the most
distant and most intimate areas reveal the mysterious bonds and
sympathies between man and the larger world: the "racing courses
of the sun" and the "loins" of the king and father (1065–66), the
powers of the underworld and the "laments in the house" (1074–79),
the private calamity and the disturbance of cities with "enmity"
(1080–83). His prophecy thus blurs that division between the familial and the political and between the upper and lower worlds that
Creon has asserted in his treatment of the corpse, his burial alive
of Antigone, his exclusively political definition of personal ties
(*philia*), and his disregard of his son's betrothal. These distinctions,
which have been the basis of his worldview, finally collapse before
his eyes when the miniature civic *epitaphios* (funeral oration) at his
entrance with Haemon's body is absorbed by the suicidal cries of
grief, curse, and lamentation within his own house.

The evocation of the *epitaphios* in the chorus' reference to Haemon as a "conspicuous memorial" in Creon's arms adds yet another
layer of meaning to the shift of lamentation from city to house. In
their study of the political ideology behind the funerary motifs in the
play, Larry Bennett and William Tyrrell have shown how Sophocles
uses two contrasting but overlapping planes of association.[2] In an
outer frame Creon is ostensibly defending the civic ethos against
the excessive demands of family. In an inner frame or subtext, however, Antigone is a figure for Athens, the idealized Athens praised
by the orators of the official funeral speeches (*epitaphioi*) pronounced at the state burial of the men who have fallen in behalf of
the city. In this inner frame Antigone embodies the courage of the
Athenians themselves as the champions of the rights of burial for
the unburied Seven warriors who fell in their attack on Thebes. This
myth, told in its most patriotic form in Euripides' *Suppliants*, underlies the political ideal of the *epitaphios* in its image of Athens: the
city acts "alone," like Antigone, to perform heroic, noble, and pious
deeds. In the play's subtext, then, Antigone is the voice of Athenian
heroism defying Theban aggression and impiety. At the end, however, our sympathies shift slightly toward Creon (which is not to say
that we excuse his harshness, folly, and stubbornness in error); and

2. Larry J. Bennett and Wm. Blake Tyrrell, "Sophocles' *Antigone* and Funeral Oratory,"
American Journal of Philology III (1990): 441–56.

he becomes the focal point of staging a miniature but failed *epitaphios*.

The inversion of Creon's attempt to commemorate his son's death as a "conspicuous memorial" parallels the inversion of his son's union with his promised bride as a marriage-in-death. As we have seen in the case of the *Trachiniae*, funerary rites and marriage rites are brought into close contact and become almost mirror images. The fusion of lament and marriage continues as Eurydice mourns the "glorious bier" or "empty bed" (depending on the text) of Creon's other son, here called Megareus (1303). The play exploits the language and gestures of civic ideology, funerary ritual, and marriage rites, but brings all of them together in complex overlappings and inversions that reach beyond the local significance of any one of these areas. These perspectives include the religiously charged spaces of the upper and lower worlds and their respective gods, the realm of unmastered nature and its gods, and the finality of death and its rituals. As in every Greek tragedy, much of the play consists of the impassioned speeches or wrenching cries of the human characters addressed to or around these numinous areas; but, as in most tragedies, they remain unmoved, and their retribution is inexorable.

* * *

In the *Antigone* too the lament of Creon is set between emotional release and disciplined restraint, and here too the contrast is expressed in terms of the difference between masculine and feminine roles; but in his case the valences are reversed. When the Messenger finishes his tale of Haemon's death, he evokes an image of moderated lament, hoping that Eurydice, in her "good judgment" (*gnōmē*) is going to keep her grief inside the house as "a domestic (or private) grief" (*oikeion penthos*) and not transgress the norms of civic behavior by unseemly screaming and wild gestures outside (1248–50). We may recall Pericles' restrictions on female presence in his Funeral Speech: women relatives are present at the tomb lamenting (*olophuromenai*, Thucydides 2.34.4); but, Pericles concludes, a woman's greatest glory is to be least talked about among men, either for praise or blame (2.45.2). Behind both the Messenger's optimism and Pericles' remark is the male-centered ethos of the polis that seeks to contain female lament inside the house as a personal and domestic woe (*penthos oikeion*) and prevent its crossing into and interfering with the public, masculine world of civic affairs, as it threatens to do, for instance, at the beginning of Aeschylus' *Seven against Thebes*.

The chorus' term "conspicuous memorial" (1258) just after Eurydice's exit continues this hope for restraint in lament. One

might expect, then, that Creon will utter a funeral speech, like that
of Peleus over Neoptolemus in Euripides' *Andromache* or Cadmus
over Pentheus in the *Bacchae*, as a "monument" for his dead son.
Contrary to such expectations, Creon's lament becomes increasingly
emotional. Whereas Eurydice suffers her grief with what the chorus hopes will be silence in public (1246–48; cf. 1251, 1256), Creon,
in public, bursts out into the threnodic cries associated with female
lamentation. Eurydice, moreover, far from keeping silent, lets out
the shrill wailing of lament (*kōkusasa*, 1302) after she "learns of her
son's suffering that deserves the shrill lament" (*oxukōkuton pathos*,
1316). She also utters curses against Creon, presumably also accompanied by emotional outcries ("And at the end she imprecated evil
fortunes upon you, killer of your sons," 1304–05).

Eurydice's lament over Haemon here echoes Antigone's lament
over Polyneices earlier (423) and uses the same verb for the shrill
wail of female keening. Creon is undone, in part, by his scorn of the
rites of the dead and specifically by his scorn of the ritual lamentation
of the dead that is the special task of women. The funerary lamentation of a woman in his house marks each stage of his defeat. His first
act in the play and in his new authority as ruler of Thebes has been
to forbid just this "wailing," as he tells the chorus in his first speech:
("that no one utter the wail of lament," 204).

The pattern of correspondence between Antigone and Eurydice
is even stronger in this scene, for Eurydice's curse on the killer of
her child echoes Antigone's curse on the one who exposed her
brother's corpse. In both cases, the one cursed is named by his
deed. Antigone "called down evil curses on those who had done
this deed" (427–428), and Eurydice "imprecated evil fortunes upon
you [Creon], killer of your sons" (1304–05). It is as if Antigone's
curse is now merging with Eurydice's, and both are being fulfilled
on the stage before our eyes.

Eurydice's curse on Creon also recalls Creon's scorn of kin ties
when he has dismissed Haemon's plea for Antigone (658–659): "So
let her make her woeful invocation [*ephumneitō*] to Zeus who
watches over kindred blood." Creon has addressed these lines to
Haemon; Eurydice echoes them at the end in cursing Creon; and
thus she reinforces the causal link between his treatment of Haemon and the ruin of his house. That ruin is now completed with this
very curse and the suicide that follows. The repeated motif of female
lamentation throughout the play becomes one of the play's main
techniques to represent the inversion of Creon's power at the end.
These laments eventually build up to the crescendo that joins Creon's own lament to the laments of women over the deaths in his own
house.

Unlike the grieving old men at the end of Euripides' *Andromache* and *Bacchae*, or even Electra in Sophocles' play, Creon's utterance is in the emotional dochmiac meter; and these are his first lyrics in the play. This lament is especially intense, moreover, because, as Creon's opening words show, he acknowledges his own guilt for the death of the son whose body he now carries (1260–69). His lament that Haemon died "by my own and not your ill counsels" (*dusbouli-ais*, 1269) harks back to the account of Haemon's death, where the Messenger generalizes about folly (*aboulia*) among men. The Messenger intends his remarks to refer primarily to the son, "showing by how much folly is set as the greatest evil for mankind" (1242–43). Now, at 1269, taking responsibility for the event, the father applies this general folly of mortals specifically to his own actions, again harking back to Teiresias' warnings (1050).

The visual tableau demonstrates the tragic situation: the father holding next to his own body the lifeless body of his son. To die thus without issue is the worst that can befall a man like Creon, and the point will be made stronger soon afterward when the Messenger mentions the death of his other son, Megareus, and reports Eurydice's dying curse on her husband as *paidoktonos*, killer of his own child (1304–05).

Had Sophocles been writing a simpler, moralizing kind of tragedy, he might have eliminated Eurydice altogether and ended the play with the first half of his closing scene, Creon confessing his guilt and error (1261–76). He could thus have concluded with the severe retributive justice pronounced by the chorus at 1270, "Alas, how you are likely to see the way of justice [*dikēn*] late, too late." Creon heavily seconds the thought, repeating the chorus' groan, "alas," *oimoi*: "Alas, I have learned, miserable that I am" (1271–72). His next lines, with their powerful metaphors of the god's "striking," "shaking," "trampling underfoot," and "overturning" all the joy in his life, vividly convey the extent of his loss and acknowledge the god's power, but do not particularly emphasize his own responsibility (1271–75): "I have learned by my misfortune; and upon my head the god then struck me with a great weight, and he drove me forth among wild roads, o woe, overturning my joy and treading it underfoot." And he concludes with a traditional gnomic utterance on the suffering of mortals (1276): "Alas, alas, the sufferings, ill-starred sufferings, of mortals."

The Second Messenger now announces another "seeing," which brings Creon to echo the chorus' moralizing statement about "seeing justice" a few lines before (1278–80): "My lord, how, as it seems, you come holding and possessing your woes: some you bear here in your hands, but others *you are soon to see in your house* when you

come." Far from bringing any sense of deep moral illumination or
sudden clarity about the shape of his life, like Heracles' "Now I
understand where I am in misfortune" in the *Trachiniae* or even
Oedipus' "Show me to all the Thebans . . . It was Apollo who fulfilled these woes," this new sight appears to Creon only as part of a
succession of woes, each worse than the last ("What still worse woe
is this again after other woes [*kakion ek kakōn eti*]?" (1281).

The man who treated Hades as merely another area of human
control enters the Hades-like tomb where he has sent Antigone.
When Ismene appealed to Antigone's imminent marriage with
Haemon, Creon dismissed her with a brutal reference to Hades'
putting an end to that marriage (575). His words now turn back
upon his own house as that marriage figuratively takes place in
Hades (1240–41): "Haemon lies there a corpse upon a corpse, having won his marriage fulfillment, miserable, in Hades' house." Having ordered his followers to "embrace" or "enfold" Antigone in her
isolated underground tomb (*tumbōi periptuxantes*, 886) out of sight
of the city to avoid the pollution of her death, Creon is now made to
witness the bloody "embrace" (*periptussetai*, 1237) that pollutes
both of the families in question with the "crimson dripping" of
blood on the "bride's" "white cheek" (1239).

The ruler who has taken pride in saving his city and acting in
behalf of the community has failed the city in its last, most vivid
hope, the communal prayer to Dionysus to "come with purifying
foot" and heal the city's disease (1140–45). "O harbor of Hades hard
to purify" is his first cry on hearing of Eurydice's death (1284). The
image cancels out his own confident image of the ship of state in
his very first lines (162–163) and renews the atmosphere of pollution that hangs over the play from its beginning, the exposed corpse
outside the walls. Creon recognizes that he has led his city into, not
out of, pollution, and that the source of that pollution is his own
house. As Teiresias has prophesied, the city has been polluted as a
result of Creon's public decrees about Polyneices' corpse (999–1022);
and so it now comes to resemble Creon's own house as a "harbor of
Hades," an interior space that is now stained with blood and increases
the existing pollutions. The Messenger's hope of ritual decorum in
that interior (1248–50) is now completely destroyed.

This change is part of an increasing tempo of emotion, violence,
and disorder. The chorus has initially visualized Creon as the "lord"
(*anax*) who "holds in his arms a conspicuous monument" (1257–58).
This description changes to Creon's own first-person statement, after
the news of Eurydice's death: "I have just now been holding my child
in my arms" (1297). He completes this outcry by another exclamation of grief and another vivid encounter with a death that he has
caused (1297–1300): "I have just now been holding my child in my

arms, alas, and yet I look at the corpse before me. Woe, woe, o unhappy mother, woe, my child." These emotional cries are like those of Antigone and Eurydice; and in fact the combination of parent and child replicates the reported lament of Eurydice immediately afterward at 1302–05. The juxtaposition here of Creon and Eurydice and of public and private space sets into relief Creon's lack of restraint and his lapse into that female emotionality that he attacked with such virulence when he was in power.

This perspective helps us better to understand the ironies in the chorus' term "conspicuous memorial" and its evocations of civic funerary speech at 1258. Creon calls his son's body a "conspicuous monument"; but, viewed in civic terms, this mourning has an ambiguous claim to such honorary and public importance. Haemon's death, to be sure, is of public concern because it deprives Creon of a male heir. Creon himself became ruler by being next of kin (174). Yet this question of succession is not particularly emphasized. As ruler in Thebes Creon is anachronistically called "king" or "lord," but also "general," *stratēgos*, suggesting the electoral procedures of fifth-century Athens alongside the hereditary succession of ancient kingship.

Having killed himself in a cave for love of a woman, Haemon has little claim to public glory. When Creon enters with the body, he addresses his dead son as "child," *pais* (1266), and later refers to him by the bare word *teknon*, "child" (1298), each time as a cry of personal, parental lament. In this latter passage, as we have observed, he brings together "mother" and "child" as he moves from the body that he has "just now" been carrying (1298) to the terrible seeing of the second body within the house, the "wretched mother" (1298–1300).

Creon repeats his painful acknowledgment of guilt with even greater intensity as he internalizes the chorus' remark that no one but he is the cause (1317–18): "Woe is me, these things will never be transferred away from my responsibility to fasten upon some other mortal." He thus repeats in his own words the chorus' accusation at the beginning of the scene (1259–60): "Here comes our lord, holding a conspicuous monument in his arms, not another's disastrous folly but his own error." Creon's repeated request at the end to be "led away" and his insistent first-person statements (*egō, emos*, I, my) now emphasize his responsibility (1319–25): "Woe is me, these things will never be transferred away from my responsibility to fasten upon some other mortal, for *I* killed you, o unhappy one, I, and this is the truth that I speak. O servants, lead me away as quickly as possible, lead me out of the way, I who am nothing more than one who is nonexistent." But at the end of his sentence this emphatically asserted first-person subject is nothing at all, literally, "one who exists no more than a no-one" (1325).

Creon continues to ask for the end of his life: he wishes never to look upon the day again (1328–33). Again the chorus replies with generalizations about the uncertainty of the future (1334–38). It closes the play with some gnomic utterances about piety, moderation, and prideful words that teach wisdom in old age (1347–53). These follow upon Creon's powerful cries of total disorientation (1343–46): "Alas, miserable me, I do not know which to look to, which way to lean [*oud' echo pros poteron idō, pāi klithō*], for everything in my hands is askew, and on the other side an unendurable destiny leapt down upon my head." Creon's last use of the verb *echein* here no longer refers to "holding" a body but to not "having" a stable place; and "everything in (his) hands" is all awry (1344–45). Creon's anguished cry at the destruction of his world will find an echo a decade or so later in Oedipus' cry at the peripeteia of the *Tyrannus* (1308–11): "Wretched that I am, where in the earth am I carried? Where does my voice flutter aloft? O you *daimōn*, where you leapt forth." Oedipus' moment of disorientation, however, conveys a very different effect, for he still has more than two hundred lines to recover his equilibrium and strength.

The ending of *Antigone* replicates the situation of the beginning of the play, but with the roles of weak and powerful, victim and agent, reversed. Creon, having misunderstood the nature of community in his "tyrannical" conception of ruling a city (733–739), performs at the end a funerary ritual in which he is virtually the sole mourner of his house. His situation, therefore, comes to mirror that of Antigone, who, in her isolated performance of the rites for Polyneices, is also the sole mourner of a ruined house. So insistent earlier on the separation of gender roles and scornful of the female (484–485, 740–741), Creon now performs the characteristically (though not exclusively) female role of lamenting over a "child" (1298–1300). Haemon's attack on his father and the suicide of Eurydice inside the house after a silent exit have already made Creon's house the mirror image of Oedipus'.

These symmetries suggest a moral order of retributive justice; and the chorus certainly interprets the action in this way in its closing lines. Yet the symmetry also keeps in view the suffering of all the individuals involved in the action. There is a cyclical repetition and perpetuation of suffering as the strong wills of Antigone and Creon clash in mutual annihilation of both houses. The chorus' moralizing "I told you so" is hardly adequate to the theatrical effect of seeing the bodies and the grieving survivors onstage.

Creon's entrance, as we have noted, prepares us for the resolution of a commemorative closure and for calming, if painful, funeral rituals in the term "conspicuous monument" for the body that he carries in his arms. Yet the expectations of a closing ceremony or a restabilizing gesture of a communal dirge *(thrēnos)* are frustrated. Instead we watch a man experiencing the total collapse of his life (however justly) and the total dissolution of meaning in his world. He neither wants to look upon the light of day (1333) nor has any stable place to "look upon" (1341–45). The chorus' closing admonition about committing no impiety against the gods does not offer much comfort, and is not meant to. It remains aloof from his grieving and does little to try to mitigate it. Here again Creon's situation mirrors Antigone's at her last appearance, for in her case too the chorus' gnomic generalizations on the limits of mortality were completely inadequate to the suffering and heroism of her situation (834–852).

Unlike Antigone, however, Creon gets what he has deserved, at least to some extent: he elicits little deep sympathy from the Theban elders whom he has intimidated and bullied (for example, 280–283). Yet the chorus' point of view need not represent the voice of the poet or the expected response of the audience. The emotionality of the scene would probably elicit some sympathy for Creon, particularly among the male spectators, who would identify with a father's loss of his last surviving son. But it also undercuts Creon's extreme valuation of civic loyalty over personal and familial ties in his definition of *philia*, the bonds of affection between individuals, as belonging entirely to the city, not to the privacy of relatives in the house (182–191). He now experiences the dissolution of those bonds of *philia* in his own house. Both his private and his public life become the very opposite of his ideals. He becomes a ruler who destroys his city by the pollutions he has brought into it (see 1015); and he becomes a father who destroys sons in a house where the wife curses the husband as the killer of his son (1302–05).

This collapse of civic order appears also in the absence of those rites of burial that have been the major concern of the play. Although Creon's entrance prepares us to expect rites of burial to close the action, these seem forgotten at the end. Indeed nothing is said of Eurydice's burial, in contrast, for instance, to the burial of Jocasta that Oedipus requests at the end of the *Tyrannus* (1446–48). The image of the community offered at the end even suggests that Thebes has not fully survived its civil war. The division between the two brothers is settled, but the royal line of Thebes is wiped out. The previous and the present ruler have each lost two sons, and neither leaves a male heir. Both leave behind pollutions in the house and in the city. In the Thebes that Creon rules, isolation replaces community, pollution replaces purification, and disorientation replaces order. If Creon's entrance with the body of Haemon, then, holds out the possibility of a reunification of the community in a collective funerary ritual, as at the end of *Ajax* or *Hippolytus* (although these

endings also have their ironies), the completion of Creon's ruin with
Eurydice's death complicates closure by leaving us with a suffering
too massive for the chorus' pious maxims in its last lines.

                              *   *   *

The shift of focus in *Antigone* from civic to domestic space is
marked by the significant detail that the Messenger describes Haemon's death not to the elders of Thebes but to Eurydice, glimpsed
for a moment in the midst of her domestic life. This circumstance
further undercuts the hope that the catastrophe of Creon's house
can be reassimilated into the masculine, political order. Eurydice is
introduced in a setting that emphasizes the contrast between public
and private space. As the Messenger arrives, the chorus sees her coming "out of the house, either because she has heard about her child or
else by chance [*tuchēi*]" (1181–82). In this gratuitous addition of
"chance," Sophocles calls attention to his own disposition of the
material. What has brought this "chance" arrival of Eurydice is, of
course, the playwright's design.

Eurydice then explains that she was just about to leave her
house—in fact, was just undoing the fastenings of the doors—to
pray to Pallas Athena when she heard "the voice of the woe from
her house" and was at once prostrated by fear (1183–89). The Messenger's report drives her back into the house. At the end of his
account, he observes that she has returned "inside the house" to
mourn "her own grief of the house" (*penthos oikeion*) among her
house-servants (*dmōais*, 1248–49). Eurydice's first words are an
address to "all the citizens" (1184), but she will grieve over her son
entirely within her domestic space. The Messenger's near-closing
phrase at 1249, *penthos oikeion stenein*, "lament over her own grief
of the house," expresses confidence that she will behave with the
restraint proper to the female behavior that males approve. It echoes
her own opening statement about "the voice of a woe concerning the
house" (*phthongos oikeiou kakou*) that struck her ears and drew her
outside (1187–88). Thus it gives the formal structure of ring composition to the little scene.

The Messenger confronting Eurydice, however, like Creon confronting Antigone, has little sense of the depths of female grief over
such "sorrow in the house" and so can hardly gauge what extremes
this grieving can reach. Whereas he speaks in general terms of
"lamenting her own grief of the house" (1249), Eurydice, much more
concretely, depicts grief as intense bodily sensation: the "voice smites
and pierces (her) ears" (*ballei di ōtōn*, 1188), and immediately she is
"struck down" and laid low by the news (*huptia klinomai . . .
apoplēssmai*, 1188–89). Her response reiterates the physical and
emotional intensity of women's grieving and especially the intensity

of their cries of mourning. When Antigone is apprehended in her crime of holy wrongdoing, she shrieks like a bird that finds its nest robbed of its young (423–428). As in Antigone's case too, the mourning of Eurydice will have a powerful corporeal effect that reaches far beyond her own grief.

In both ancient and modern Greece, the death of a son on the verge of marriage is the most painful imaginable loss and the one most likely to arouse the greatest mourning. Hence Eurydice's maternal grief expresses the most disturbing and dangerous form of female lament. It requires little experience of grieving mothers in Greece, to say nothing of Greek tragedy, to realize how far off the mark are the Messenger's closing words about restrained grieving (1246–50). In keeping the mourning over the city's hero, Eteocles, separate from any rites for the city's traitor, Polyneices, Creon has attempted essentially the same strategy as the Messenger, but on a larger scale. The Messenger's report of Eurydice's death, after her violent cries of lamentation and imprecation, destroys any remaining hope of his success.

The totality of Eurydice's involvement in her maternity is underlined by her epithet, "all-mother of the corpse" of her son (*pammētōr nekrou,* 1282), the mother in the fullest sense, to the fullest possible extent, "whose grief for her son," as Jebb remarks, "would not suffer her to survive him." Thus her shrieks and curses culminate in the unusually bloody suicide, "with freshly cutting blows" "beneath the liver" (1283–84, 1315). The wild cries of the dirge or wailing (1247) are traditionally accompanied by tearing of the hair and rending of cheeks and breast. Eurydice, like other wildly grieving women in tragedy, takes those gestures of physical self-harming to their most extreme conclusion.

Athens had long sought to keep such extreme expressions of grief under state control; and the official funeral speech (*epitaphios*), pronounced by a male magistrate over male warriors in civic space, was (among its other functions) one of the major forms of such control in the latter half of the fifth century. As Nicole Loraux has emphasized, there is a deep cultural conflict between the *thrēnos* (lament) of women and the *epitaphios*, a conflict that closely parallels the struggle between Antigone and Creon in Sophocles' play.[3] That antagonism is played out in miniature in the closing scene. The desperate suicidal gesture of the grieving mother inside the house overwhelms the chorus' initial attempt to subsume the son's death into the masculine commemoration of a "conspicuous memorial." The anguish of the female cry of mourning, the *goos*, to which the

3. Nicole Loraux, *The Invention of Athens: The Funeral Oration in the Classical City,* trans. Alan Sheridan (Cambridge, MA: Harvard UP, 1986).

Messenger alludes in his closing hopes of its restraint (1247), cannot in fact be kept confined within female space and apart from the
public life of the city. As the king himself says, "a woman's death"
now comes heaped on the present slaughter; and the elders of the
chorus reply, "It is there to see and no longer inside the inner cham-
bers [*muchoi*] of the house" (1291–93). Creon's own cries of woe as
he holds the body of his son are, in many places, indistinguishable
from the cries of female wailing (for example, 1266–68, 1306–11).

                              *   *   *

   This closing movement, therefore, replays the central conflicts of
the action but on very different ground. The issue of controlling lamentation and funerary rites has focused on the city, on politics, and
on public space. In deciding who should receive burial, Creon
attempted to assert the city's claims over those of house and family.
The latter fall to women, who traditionally perform the lament over
the dead, wash and lay out the body, and are involved in the intimate, physical contact with the corpse—a contact that Antigone
alone has experienced in her defiant care for the corpse of her
brother. The men of the city who constitute the chorus try in their
last utterances to pull the discourse back to "doing," "taking care"
of what needs care, thinking, and teaching. But Creon, in contrast
to his earlier confrontations with the women of his house, is now
without counsel or direction (1339–47).
   This pull between ritual and gnomic closure on the one hand and
anticlosural elements on the other is characteristic of Sophoclean
endings: the *Ajax* and *Oedipus at Colonus* are particularly clear
examples. The ritual lament brings a formal closure; yet the uncon-
soled loss—on the part of Tecmessa, Teucer, and the Salaminian
chorus in *Ajax*, or of Oedipus' still grieving daughters in the
Colonus—keeps the suffering from full resolution and so holds it
still in the realm of the tragic. Through such endings tragedy places
before us a vision of the world as a place of potential chaos and
threatens the human need for order, hope, and reasonableness. Yet
tragedy—Greek, Elizabethan, or contemporary—rarely suggests that
chaos is the final result. The justice of Creon's end and his own
acknowledgment of his responsibility vindicate Antigone and leave
us with that punitive justice of the gods of which Teiresias has
warned. This seems enough for the Theban elders, who close the play
with their gnomic pronouncement: "To have good sense is the first
part of happiness; and one must commit no impiety against the gods.
The big words of those who are proud to excess, paying back big
blows as the price, have taught good sense in old age." Yet three
innocent people have died, one precisely because of her piety
toward the gods; and two are far from old age. Neither these losses

nor the intensity of Creon's suffering—to say nothing of Eurydice's—
can be assimilated into the comfortable moral explanation with
which the chorus ends.

BETINE VAN ZYL SMIT

Antigone Enters the Modern World[†]

The Archive of Performances of Greek and Roman Drama in Oxford
has 142 performances of Sophocles' *Antigone* or new versions of it
on record for the twenty-first century alone. This indicates the continued engagement of creative artists with the drama and makes it
impossible to give an adequate overview in one chapter of the part
this tragedy has played in modern cultural life. Fortunately scholars and reviewers have also been busy in recording their research
on and criticism of *Antigone* and its multitude of descendants.[1]

The modern Antigone, fearless champion of traditional piety and
family loyalty, a bold rebel, defying tyrannical rule, springs from the
way Sophocles shaped the myth in his tragedy. This chapter examines
the way in which *Antigone* was re-imagined over the centuries, but
concentrates on two recent adaptations that give a good indication
of the importance this play still has in modern culture. *The Island,*
first created by Athol Fugard, John Kani and Winston Ntshona in
apartheid South Africa in 1973, with its play-within-the-play *The
Trial and Punishment of Antigone*, has become a classic in the modern world to depict resistance to authoritarian rule.[2] *Antigone in
Molenbeek*, written by the Flemish author Stefan Hertmans and
first performed in 2016, responds to the contemporary crisis of cultural and religious conflict in Europe and the modern world.
Attention is also paid to the way different nuances were brought to
the conflict between Creon and Antigone in early modern Europe,
the stimulus of the pioneering production in 1841 in Prussian Potsdam, which was to find echoes in France, England, Ireland and the
Czech lands. Another most influential adaptation was that of Jean
Anouilh in occupied Paris in 1944. In spite of its ambivalent treatment of the two central characters, it in turn spawned new versions
which established Antigone as a symbol of heroic resistance to tyranny, and also a feminist icon.

---

† From *Looking at Antigone*, ed. David Stuttard (London: Bloomsbury Academic, 2018),
pp. 157–69. © Betine van Zyl Smit, 2018, Bloomsbury Academic, an imprint of Bloomsbury
Publishing Plc. Reprinted with permission. Unless otherwise indicated, notes are by the
author. Some of the author's notes have been omitted.
1. See the section on later reception in the Selected Bibliography [*Editor's note*].
2. *The Island* is excerpted in this Norton Critical Edition, pp. 50–55 [*Editor's note*].

Early Modern Antigones

The confrontation of Creon and Antigone in Sophocles' tragedy has been reinterpreted in different ways in later literature. Sometimes Creon is represented as a tyrant. Antigone is sometimes a loyal family supporter or a doomed romantic. Many early modern versions take Ismene's decision not to oppose Creon's decree as the right one.

Early modern playwrights and scholars were intrigued by the conflict between Creon and Antigone and its moral ambivalences and the complexity of the character of Antigone, who can be judged, in Sophocles' version, to be an uncompromising protagonist as well as an innocent victim, at moments fierce and then pathetic, defiant and sufficiently heroic to face death. Many of the early modern scholars and translators interpreted the play as a lesson about the abuse of power, and made Creon a tyrant, who suffers the punishment he deserves for his stubbornness and pride. During the early modern period, when Greek tragedy was rediscovered by the Humanists, few people could read Classical Greek, and the Greek dramas were often translated into Latin. Several such translations were made in the sixteenth century. Robert Miola explains how some of the translators used words that altered the emphases of the Greek version and ended up offering a new interpretation.[3] The word *tyrannus* for a ruler tended to be interpreted in the modern sense of tyrant, and Creon often became an evil ruler and the direct opposite of the just ruler, which was the ideal of many philosophical discourses of the time. The great Humanist Erasmus was one of the scholars who saw Creon in *Antigone* as the incarnation of a bad ruler: 'Creon . . . who preferred to obey his own mind rather than wise counsels and destroyed utterly his family and himself.' He calls him a tyrant and not a prince. Erasmus read *Antigone* as a story of deserved punishment, an object lesson against tyranny, obstinacy and impiety.

Haemon was often re-imagined as a romantic lead who died for love. Sophocles' Antigone does not show a great deal of interest in love or her husband-to-be. Haemon's suicide is motivated not just by his love for Antigone, but also by rage at his father's stubborn inflexibility.

One of the earliest adaptations of Sophocles' *Antigone* was the 1580 version by the French playwright Robert Garnier with the title *Antigone, ou la Piété*. Garnier, a precursor of the Classical French tragedians Corneille and Racine, combined elements of Seneca's *Phoenissae*, Statius' *Thebaid* and Sophocles' tragedy to create a very long play with resonances of contemporary French politics. The

---

3. Robert S. Miola, "Early Modern Antigones: Receptions, Refractions, Replays," *Classical Receptions Journal* 6 (2014): 230.

drama includes the part of the myth where Oedipus is still alive, covers the war between Eteocles and Polyneices and contains a version of Sophocles' *Antigone* as the last two acts, lines 1516–2741. Scholars have analysed the play as portraying contemporary dynastic and religious civil wars in France and the prospect of tyrannical rule. Garnier's Antigone is pious, as the title indicates, but she is an eloquent and powerful character. She instructs Creon on the limits of royal power and the subordination of human to divine law:

> Nulles loix de Tyrans ne doivent avoir lieu
> Que lon voit repugner aux preceptes de Dieu.
>
> 1814–5
> [No Tyrants' laws should contradict the teachings of God.]

There are echoes of the traditional Catholic teaching in the play. The conflicting claims of secular and religious authority in France at the time undoubtedly provide a large part of the context for Garnier's interpretation. It is clear that such versions, where Creon becomes an uncompromising tyrant, lose much of the subtle ambiguities of the interplay between ruler and subject about secular and religious duties, which are part of the Greek tragedy.

Such one-sided interpretations were, however, not the only way Sophocles' *Antigone* was viewed in later years.

Antigone in Potsdam (1841)

During the nineteenth century German scholars were hard at work researching Greek tragedy in all its aspects, from textual correctness to the way the plays were staged in the ancient world. When the relatively young Friedrich Wilhelm IV became King of Prussia in 1840, this academic work was rewarded by being given the opportunity to be translated into practice. The new ruler enjoyed the reputation of being a romantic aesthete and was expected to inaugurate a period of liberalism. As crown prince the King had already shown a fondness for the arts and sciences and he was in the forefront of those who subscribed to the spirit of philhellenism, which imagined the Germans as destined to re-embody classical Greece. It was the King himself who shaped the plan to produce historically accurate performances of Greek tragedy. Sophocles' *Antigone* was chosen as the first play for this bold initiative.

The staging of *Antigone* in Potsdam in 1841 became widely regarded as epoch-making. It was exported all over Europe and considered as the model for a revival and totally new reincarnation of Greek tragedy. This opened a new chapter in the discourse on theatre. A follower of the Romantic school, Ludwig Tieck, was chosen for the task. The project was to be based on the latest research. The text used was a new verse translation by Johann Jakob Christian Donner. A leading scholar of Greek who was an exponent of the historical critical approach, August Böckh, was appointed as philological adviser. The theatrical space inside the *Neue Palais* in Potsdam was adapted to conform to the archaeological knowledge of the time as displayed in the famous study *Das Theater von Athen* by Hans Christian Genelli (1818). This knowledge in fact soon became outdated as a result of the findings of the new excavations of the theatre of Dionysus in Athens that started at the time of the performance.

The classicistic conception entailed the division of the stage into three levels: a subterranean level for the musicians; a slightly higher orchestra level, where the Chorus of fifteen and their leader moved and which also housed the altar of Dionysus (in which the prompt was concealed), in the centre; the raised stage formed the third level, 1.5 metres above, and represented the palace. The young Felix Mendelssohn-Bartholdy was commissioned to provide the choral music. He chose a romantic oratorio and symphonic style to set Donner's verse with great virtuosity as well as accuracy regarding the metre, as advised by Böckh. Mendelssohn soon became the driving force of the production. This innovative theatrical project combined historicism, Romantic notions and an attempt to convey an aspect of antiquity adequately. This was important for a theatre that set itself the task to serve as a 'cultural memory'.

Tieck tended to Christian interpretations, in the case of Antigone portraying her as a martyr. Dionysus was readily identified as Christ by the Romantics. At the same time this staging acknowledged the implicit relationship between Antigone and Dionysus that was long ignored by researchers. In this romantic fashion the appeal to the god to appear, which in Sophocles' tragedy is only indicated symbolically, was acted out as an epiphany in the theatre:

> come to us
> > dionysus
> come with your
> > cleansing step

trans. Stuttard

Mendelssohn had reworked the ecstatic fifth stasimon[4] as a call for help addressed to the god of the theatre to appear. Anton Bierl has argued persuasively that the scene was 'patently tailored to refer to the new king himself who had been for some time representing an equally Romantic Dionysus cult infused with Christianity in the

---

4. The choral ode at lines 1116–52 [*Editor's note*].

architectural symbolism of Charlottenburg castle'.[5] Friedrich Wilhelm IV was thus represented as a moral force in that he and the god were associated in the quest for purification. Creon is portrayed as having to bear the guilt of Antigone's death.

Sophocles' *Antigone* had not been staged in Britain during the seventeenth and eighteenth centuries, except as adapted in the Italian opera of Francesco Bianchi in 1796. One of the reasons for the absence of *Antigone* may have been that there was no example of a recent French version of the play. It is significant that an English translation of the tragedy *Antigone*, which was produced at Covent Garden in 1845, was largely derived from the famous production in Potsdam in 1841. The London *Antigone* made use of the music Mendelssohn had composed and was further indebted to the Prussian production in its use of the German translation of Donner, rendered into English by William Bartholomew. The choice of this production may in part have been a tribute to Queen Victoria's marriage in 1841 to Prince Albert, who was an admirer of the cultural renewal at the Prussian court. The turn to German rather than French examples of the staging of Greek plays signalled a new source of inspiration for the British stage. The London production also reflected the awakening interest in archaeological and antiquarian studies at the time. Both costumes and set were products of careful research. This is but one of many examples of how different performances and adaptations of Sophocles' tragedy in their turn provoked new versions.

Jean Anouilh *Antigone,* Paris, 1944

One of the most influential modern reworkings of Sophocles' tragedy is that of the French playwright, Jean Anouilh. It was staged for the first time during the German occupation of France, on 4 February 1944. While many saw it as expressing French defiance to the Germans, Antigone embodying the French resistance and saying 'no' to German rule, Anouilh actually managed to preserve much of the ambiguity of the Greek drama. Some French intellectuals attacked Anouilh's interpretation, charging him with creating a Créon whose attitude was an insult to the many who had died in resisting the Germans.

In spite of the ambivalence of critical and scholarly reception of Anouilh's intentions, many subsequent adaptors of the play continued to see his Antigone as a modern incarnation of defiance to tyrannical rule. One of the most famous instances of this reception

5. Anton Bierl, "Germany, Austria, and Switzerland," in *Handbook to the Reception of Greek Drama,* ed. Betine van Zyl Smit (Malden, MA: Wiley-Blackwell, 2016), p. 263.

is *The Island*, a play created by the South African trio of Athol
Fugard, John Kani and Winston Ntshona. Athol Fugard particularly mentioned the parallel circumstances in which these two plays
were first presented: Anouilh's version in Paris with German officers sitting in the theatre enjoying French culture, while in South
Africa, when *The Island* was first performed in Cape Town in
1973, there were three Special Branch officers present in the
audience. They were ready to arrest and prosecute the actors and
director if the play was deemed to break the law as defined under
the State of Emergency in South Africa at the time. This did not
happen, and *The Island* went on to tour the stages of the world. It
has become one of the adaptations of Sophocles' drama that best
encapsulates fearless resistance to an oppressive state.

The Island by Athol Fugard, John Kani and Winston Ntshona

This play grew out of the work of a group of amateur Black actors
who had come to the playwright and theatre director, Athol Fugard,
for help at his home in Port Elizabeth in the 1960s. Previously, in
the early twentieth century, Sophocles' *Antigone* had been performed
in South Africa by White cultural organizations as an example of
Western high culture. No fewer than three translations into Afrikaans of the tragedy had been published and performed. This was
at least partly aimed at validating the language of the Afrikaners who
were striving for self-realization in the face of English cultural
hegemony after the defeat of their forebears in the Anglo-Boer War
of 1899–1902. Performances of these Afrikaans translations had
eschewed any overt application of Antigone's act of defiance to the
situation in South Africa. Gradually, however, from the early 1960s
Antigone was to be given a new lease of life in the Black Theatre of
the townships and was eventually to be one of the plays that brought
Black protest theatre to the attention of White audiences too. The
impact went beyond the decision to stage versions of *Antigone,* and
led to a deeper examination of Antigone as a figure who resists
authority. This examination in turn caused a shift in the moral
balance between the characters, with sympathies moving clearly
towards Antigone.

Various township theatre groups staged productions of *Antigone*
in the 1960s. It was one of the plays Athol Fugard rehearsed with
the Serpent Players, a group in New Brighton, outside Port Elizabeth. They were constantly harassed by the police and often members were arrested. Fugard did eventually succeed in producing
Antigone with the Serpent Players in 1965, but he was unable to

attend the performance as he was refused the permit needed by a
White person to attend a Non-white gathering.

A further development of this project of the Serpent Players was
that one of the actors involved, Norman Ntshinga, who was to play
Haemon, but was arrested before the performance, actually put on
a two-man version of *Antigone* with another Serpent player, Sipho
'Sharkey' Mguqulwa, in prison on Robben Island. They used work-
shop techniques and relied on their memory of the play they were
rehearsing before their arrest.

This was not the only time *Antigone* was performed in the maxi-
mum security jail for political prisoners on Robben Island. In his
autobiography President Nelson Mandela deals briefly with what he
refers to as his 'thespian career':

> Our amateur drama society made its yearly offering at Christ-
> mas. My thespian career . . . had a modest revival on Robben
> Island. Our productions were what might now be called mini-
> malist: no stage, no scenery, no costumes. All we had was the
> text of the play.
>
> I performed in only a few dramas, but I had one memorable
> role: that of Creon, the king of Thebes in Sophocles' *Antigone*.
> I had read some of the classic Greek plays in prison, and found
> them enormously elevating. What I took out of them was that
> character was measured by facing up to difficult situations and
> that a hero was a man who would not break down even under
> the most trying circumstances.
>
> When *Antigone* was chosen as the play, I volunteered my
> services, and was asked to play Creon, an elderly king fighting
> a civil war over the throne of his beloved city-state. At the out-
> set, Creon is sincere and patriotic, and there is wisdom in his
> early speeches when he suggests that experience is the foun-
> dation of leadership and that obligation to the people takes pre-
> cedence over loyalty to an individual . . .
>
> But Creon deals with his enemies mercilessly. He has
> decreed that the body of Polyneices, Antigone's brother, who
> had rebelled against the city, does not deserve a proper burial.
> Antigone rebels, on the grounds that there is a higher law than
> that of the state. Creon will not listen to Antigone, neither
> does he listen to anyone but his own inner demons. His inflex-
> ibility and blindness ill become a leader, for a leader must tem-
> per justice with mercy. It was Antigone who symbolized our
> struggle; she was, in her own way, a freedom fighter, for she
> defied the law on the ground that it was unjust.

President Mandela's criticism of Creon's fatal flaw, his inflexibility,
and his judgement that a leader should temper justice with mercy,

were to be put into practice when he, as President of South Africa after the first fully democratic elections in the country in 1994, followed a policy of reconciliation. This was a decisive rejection of Creon's approach to governing his state. President Mandela's view of Antigone as a heroine in the struggle for justice encapsulates the interpretation of this role by Black South African theatre activists from the 1960s onwards. There is no trace of the ambivalence in scholarly debate about the roles of Creon and Antigone; for Black theatre in South Africa, she was constantly presented as a martyr and a heroine.

The appeal that Antigone's defiance had for the Black majority in South Africa, who were oppressed by laws that ran contrary to the spirit of justice and humanity, found its finest expression in a play devised by two new members of the Serpent Players, again in collaboration with Athol Fugard. This play was first staged in Cape Town under the title *Die Hodoshe Span* at a multi-racial private theatre called The Space, on 2 July 1973. The play was directed by Athol Fugard and his two collaborators, John Kani and Winston Ntshona, formed the cast, John and Winston. Under its final title, *The Island*, the term used colloquially to refer to the jail on Robben Island, the play was destined to take around the world the identification of the South African struggle with Antigone's refusal to bow to tyranny.

The play is set in a prison cell on Robben Island. The two inmates, John and Winston, are rehearsing for the annual prison concert, a two-man version of *Antigone*. John is the director. He produces the dialogue from memory as they have no script. Their props are homemade and rudimentary. They have been disempowered by a ruthless regime, and just like Antigone, a defenceless woman, they have only words to defend their cause. The plot is couched in terms familiar to convicts: it is the trial of Antigone, the accused is Antigone, the state, king Creon, and the charge is that Antigone buried Polyneices. Significantly he is referred to by John as 'the traitor, the one who I said was on our side' (p. 201).

They also reminisce about the production of *Antigone* by the Serpent players in Port Elizabeth in 1965. Thus they incorporate the lived experience of their theatre group into the play. John presents stage one of the trial thus: 'The State lays charges against the Accused . . . and lists counts . . . you know the way they do it. Stage two is Pleading. What does Antigone plead? Guilty or Not Guilty?' Winston instinctively replies: 'Not Guilty.' John reacts with: 'Now look, Winston, we're not going to argue. Between me and you, in this cell, we know she's Not Guilty. But in the play she pleads Guilty.' (p. 201). Winston maintains that Antigone is not guilty because she had every right to bury her brother. Winston reluctantly bows to

John's insistence that he has to accept the wording of the play, but later Winston wants to say that Antigone lays charges against the state. This underlines his passionate conviction of the rightness of her cause.

They summarize the rest of the play as:

| John | Stage three: Pleading in Mitigation of Sentence. Stage four. |
| **Winston** | State summary, Sentence and Farewell Words. |

p. 203

When they have their 'dress rehearsal' and Winston has to try on the improvised wig and false breasts, John's laughter incenses Winston. He vows that he will not play 'a bloody woman' and expose himself to the ridicule of his fellow prisoners:

> 'Go to hell man. Only last night you tell me that this Antigone is a bloody . . . what you call it . . . legend! A Greek one at that. Bloody thing never even happened. Not even history! Look brother, I got no time for bullshit. Fuck legends. Me . . . I live my life here! I know why I'm here, and it's history, not legends. I had my chat with a magistrate in Cradock and now I'm here. Your Antigone is child's play, man.'

p. 210

The coarse, everyday language of *The Island*, often mixed with Xhosa and Afrikaans words, is in contrast with the elevated style of Greek tragedy and the way it was usually presented in South Africa, whether in English or Afrikaans translation. This language of ordinary people made the play accessible to everybody.

When the play-within-the-play is staged, when John and Winston put on *The Trial and Punishment of Antigone,* Winston's gradual identification with Antigone and her conviction highlights the theme of the play so that every member of the audience understands it. The final scene of *The Island* is the prison concert. *The Island*'s audience becomes the prison audience when John addresses them: 'Captain Prinsloo, Hodoshe, warders . . . and Gentlemen!' (p. 223). The last term is reserved for his fellow prisoners and accords them the dignity and respect they do not get in prison. John gives a brief synopsis of the background of *Antigone*. He then changes into his Creon costume and in that role makes a speech. The adoption of the fictive character gives him licence to send up the rhetoric of the South African regime with sly references to 'constant troubles on our borders', 'subversive elements' (p. 224) and so forth.

Winston then appears, dressed as Antigone, and is charged with having buried Polyneices. He pleads guilty. Given the opportunity to plead in mitigation Winston, like Antigone, asserts that there is a higher law than that of the state. This law comes from God. The dialogue in the play carries a triple layer of meaning: it represents Winston and John acting the words of Antigone and Creon in the Greek drama, but the ideas expressed apply equally to the position of Winston and John in *The Island* as well as to the conviction of Fugard, Ntshona and Kani in the reality of South Africa in the 1970s. This becomes explicit when John as Creon pronounces sentence: 'Take her from where she stands, straight to the Island.' This identification of Winston with Antigone and consequently of *The Island* with *Antigone* is underscored in Winston's last words:

> Brothers and Sisters of the Land! I go now on my last journey. I must leave the light of day forever, for the Island, strange and cold, to be lost between life and death. So to my grave, my everlasting prison, condemned alive to solitary death.
>
> p. 227

But then Winston goes beyond the role of Antigone. He strips off his wig and confronts the audience as Winston:

> Nyana we Sizwe! [Son of the Land]
> Gods of our Fathers! My Land! My home!
> Time waits no longer. I go now to my living death, because
>   I honoured
> those things to which honour belongs.

Thus he movingly declares his own renewed defiance before he is returned to his existence of serving punishment for daring to resist laws that are manifestly unjust. The impact of Winston's words is enhanced by the reversal of his earlier vehement refusal to play Antigone, a Greek legend, a bloody woman, child's play. His realization of the deeper meaning of her defiance thus underlines the convergence of the ideals that Antigone represents and those of the protesters against the unjust laws of the apartheid state.

While *Antigone* has a beginning, a middle and an end, *The Island*, has a ring composition. The play opens with the two prisoners caught in a Sisyphean task of endlessly filling a wheelbarrow with sand, wheeling it to a different spot, emptying it, filling it up again and wheeling it back. The convicts are shackled together and beaten. This brutal action to which they return after their performance puts into sharp relief the human dignity expressed in Antigone's last words with which they are completely identified at the end of the play. Outwardly the positions of John and Winston are the same at the end of *The Island* as at the beginning, but change has been brought about in the audience's perception of them. Anonymous prisoners at the outset, the audience now knows them intimately. In the course of staging *The Trial and Punishment of Antigone* they have revealed themselves as human beings, who are undergoing a living death because of their beliefs in a higher justice. Their cause is the same as that of Antigone. The words spoken by the actors, by the prisoners, assert their humanity and transport them and their fictive audience, their fellow Robben Island convicts, beyond the reach of a repressive regime. *The Island* is a brilliant celebration of the power of Greek tragedy and the theatre to transcend obstacles and to give voice to the voiceless.

Another recent adaptation of *Antigone* has attempted to focus attention on the plight of families who are similarly marginalized and have become the collateral damage in terrorist attacks in Europe.

Stefan Hertmans *Antigone in Molenbeek*, 2016

After the terrorist attacks in Paris in November 2015 and in Brussels in March 2016, attention was focused on Molenbeek, a suburb of Brussels with which many of the *jihadists* associated with these attacks had a connection. Some had lived there for a number of years, or still lived there, and much of the planning for their attacks had probably been done there. In an attempt to find answers to the question of why such an area should have become a breeding ground for terror, a cultural event, 'Re:Creating Europe', was organized in Amsterdam in June 2016. Central questions to be considered were how authors or playwrights could react to the attacks. What could they say about them? And on whose behalf would they be speaking? For this occasion the Flemish author, Stefan Hertmans, wrote a theatre monologue, *Antigone in Molenbeek*. It was staged in the Bellevue Theatre in Amsterdam and the full text was published in a supplement to the Belgian newspaper *De Standaard* on 3 June 2016. This play is a thought-provoking exploration of how the central conflict in *Antigone* can still shed light on some of the cardinal issues in contemporary multi-cultural societies.

The link to Sophocles' *Antigone* is in the title of the one-act play. The Antigone of this contemporary adaptation is a young Moroccan woman, Nouria. She goes to the police station to claim the body of her brother who has been killed. The dour policeman, to whom she addresses her request, is the representative of the state and thus has the Creon role. He is 'Meneer' (Mister) Crénom. Nouria is proud of her Belgian passport and is a law student in Brussels. She has become part of the contemporary world where she lives. Production photographs show her in modern Western dress, not in the garments prescribed by some Muslim communities.

The police officer's role is more limited than that of Creon. He has not made the law, but he has to enforce it. Nouria's mission, however, is very close to that of Antigone. She wants to retrieve her brother's remains from the state so that they may be given proper religious burial. It becomes clear that her brother's body is no longer a body, but remains in the literal sense. Crénom even speaks of 'material'. This seems to point to the result of suicide bombing and is reminiscent of Anouilh's Créon's telling Antigone that the remains of Polynice and Etéocle were so intermingled that they could not be distinguished.

In contrast to most Antigones, however, Nouria is timid and nervous. Nevertheless she insists on referring to her brother's remains as 'mijn broer', my brother, not 'Het Materiaal'. The insistence on his humanity is part of her resistance to the official approach. Crénom is drawn not without sympathy, as a bumbling official who has to toe the line. Only when he feels under pressure does he describe Nouria's brother as an enemy of the state and also a traitor to his own community. He also spells it out that her brother is practically now no more than a dossier, that there really is not a shred of his body that is whole. But Nouria insists. She is familiar with the view of body bags after a terrorist incident and persists that his remains must be somewhere, perhaps in a bag in a fridge.

There is a moment of metatheatre when Nouria speculates that her brother may be lying above ground somewhere, rotting and as prey to crows and worms. This immediately brings to mind Sophocles' opening scene where Antigone tells Ismene about the fate of the brothers, especially ll. 26–30 (But Polyneices . . . Polyneices' poor dead corpse . . . They say that Creon has had it broadcast publicly that no one is to bury him or mourn him. No! But they're to leave him there unwept, unburied, so much carrion for birds to glut on' [trans. Stuttard]). Crénom's reaction, that this is no theatre, reinforces the link.

As Nouria becomes more emotional, the officer becomes more brutal. His initial restraint in referring to the young man is replaced by strong condemnation of him as an enemy of a tolerant society, a young man who embraced terror and random violence. Nouria's appeal that he was her beloved brother and that the officer should try to imagine losing his brother or sister is met with indignation and sarcasm—does Nouria perhaps want a state funeral for her brother? Nouria is sent away with the vague promise that if any news should become available she will be summoned.

More information about Nouria's family background is given. Her father has become blind and disappeared, thus assimilating him to Oedipus. Her brother used to be a keen football player, goalkeeper, but an accident in which he injured his head led to him abandoning the sport and eventually leaving for a foreign country, from where he sent a 'selfie' against a background of desert sand and black flags. These are the familiar marks of terrorist organizations. On his return to Belgium he was changed. This sketches the story familiar in contemporary media of young men of Muslim families who have grown up in European countries, but leave for terrorist training in camps in the Middle East. In this way the story of Nouria and her brother becomes the story of many other families in modern multi-cultural Europe. Nouria is not executed. That is not the way the modern state deals with family loyalty, but she is left bereft. The modern Creon, the state, is also left unpunished for its treatment of the family. This suggests the intractability of the problem of dealing with the clash between the two cultures. Both end up by losing.

This stripped-down version of Sophocles nevertheless succeeds in deploying the conflict at the heart of the Greek tragedy to express one of the most pressing problems in the world today. It takes its place in the line of countless other transformations of *Antigone* to draw attention to contemporary issues.

HELENE FOLEY

The Voices of Antigone[†]

* * *

When Sophocles wrote this play, we think that he knew that many in Athens would not accept burying a traitor in Athenian territory and there may at some point have been a law passed to this effect. (It is not clear whether this law would have permitted burial outside Athens to avoid pollution.) If so, Sophocles needed to create an unusually persuasive as well as dangerous voice for Antigone, a voice far more individualized and unusual than those of other tragic characters. At least in extant tragedy, there is no voice in other Greek tragedies like hers, whereas we can find precedents for the voices of the other characters in other plays. Her atypical female identity, her attempt to adapt and make comprehensible her dissenting mode of ethical deliberation, and her terrible situation seem to be part of her attraction to later playwrights and composers and to philosophers and psychoanalytic thinkers like Georg Wilhelm Friedrich Hegel,

† From *Looking at Antigone*, ed. David Stuttard (London: Bloomsbury Academic, 2018), pp. 150–56. © Helene Foley 2018, Bloomsbury Academic, an imprint of Bloomsbury Publishing Plc. Reprinted with permission. The author's notes have been omitted.

Martin Heidegger, Søren Kierkegaard, Jacques Lacan, Judith Butler and others.

In later dramatic versions of *Antigone*, however, the heroine develops a wide range of powerful voices. If Sophocles' heroine establishes a unique voice, in contemporary South America she can represent a multitude of lamenting and resisting female voices who want to learn the truth about the thousands of disappeared and unburied victims of dictatorial regimes and to lament and memorialize those dead and tortured. In a play called *Antígona oriental* directed and composed by Marianella Morena with the German director Volker Lösch performed at the Teatro Solis in Montevideo, Uruguay, in 2012, Antigone was played by one professional actress and nineteen female survivors of imprisonment and torture during Uruguay's 1973–75 dictatorship. Even Ismene becomes Antigone in the course of the play. The victims wanted the current democratic left-wing government not to repress the ugly past, but to remember it and respond to its injustices, such as the amnesty granted to the military in 1986. The play interwove real-life testimonies from the survivors with Sophocles' text; but these individual testimonies became a shared story of all the Antigones. This play gives Antigone's courage to all of these women and makes heroines and agents out of victims. At the surprising conclusion of this new version, the play's Creons offer an offstage apology and the twenty women enter the stage dressed in festal red attire, dancing, and recording their desire for a space to move on and survive:

> Sophocles, I beg you
> Send me an ending
> In which someone is saved
> So that we can start again.

In South America, innumerable new versions of *Antigone* preceded this production. In Griselda Gambaro's seminal 1986 *Antígona furiosa* in Buenos Aires, Antigone became the voice of all the sisters, mothers and daughters who suffered death, disappearance, or losses during the Argentinian dictatorship of 1976–83 that caused more than 30,000 people, including many young people, to disappear. In response to these disappearances, a group of mothers and grandmothers bravely began marching in protest in 1977 on the central public square of the Plaza de Mayo, a location linked with Argentine independence and public transparency, to demand news of their loved ones and the return of missing bodies for burial. Later they continued to object to insufficient response to the perpetrators of injustice and to the continued silence about and failure to adequately memorialize the many disappeared.

This play begins with the dead Antigona coming back to life still in prison. After furiously re-enacting the fratricidal battle between her siblings, marching like the mothers of the Plaza de Mayo, symbolically performing the burial of her brother, and refusing the belated pardon of Creon until all the dead are buried, she commits suicide once again: 'I will always want to bury Polynices. Even if I am born 1,000 times, and he dies 1,000 times.' Two other characters, Corifeo (his name means Chorus-leader) and Antinoo (meaning anti-mind) play the denizens of a modern café who observe Antigona. They sometimes mock Antigona—'You will descend free and alive to death. It is not so tragic!'—and sometimes adopt both the role of Creon, who is represented as an empty shell that they put on, or other characters, even the dead Polynices. Antigona herself briefly takes on the roles of Ismene and Haemon. In the end, Antinoo confirms that Antigona herself has become one of the disappeared who always reappears: 'She is here and she is not here, we killed her and we did not kill her . . . What a bore! She never ends it! . . . If we know she dies, why doesn't she die?'

Among many other South and Central American *Antigones*, the 2004 Mexican *Las voces que incendian el desierto* ('The Voices that Set the Desert on Fire') by Perla de la Rosa similarly addressed the 'femicide' of actual women in Ciudad Juárez. In this play three pairs of women, including the sisters Antigone and Ismene, search for missing sisters or daughters. If in Latin America Antigone often becomes a collective figure that insists on burying and memorializing many historical dead, in other countries she can adopt a different pointedly individual voice. A 2004 Japanese production of a new version of *Antigone* by Miyagi Satoshi's Ku Na'uka Theatre Company in Tokyo deployed Antigone's intense individuality to encourage his audience to develop a non-conformist voice that could challenge a state authority still too devoted to aspects of pre–Second World War nationalism and outdated social mores. In this play a Chorus of multiple timid and obedient Ismenes represented (especially female) citizens who prefer to compromise with the legacy of the past rather than directly confronting power embodied by multiple patriarchal Creons. Only Antigone and Haemon stood outside these groups.

Staging the play in front of the National Museum of Japan, built in 1930 as a monument to Japanese nationalism, allowed the production to address symbolically the entire country. Stage left served as the entrance for women and represented nature and blood bonds and the western world of the dead, stage right served as the entrance for men and presented political authority. Haemon, however, linked himself with democracy by entering from the audience itself; he avoided the gruff and threatening language and gestures of the Creons. Antigone refused to use feminine Japanese, performed the burial of Polynices on stage, and walked under her own volition into the structure at centre stage that represented the cave in which she removed her black kimono before committing suicide accompanied by drums and other musical instruments and then donned a white robe appropriate for a wedding or death. Miyagi's feminist version removed those parts of Sophocles' text that criticized the heroine and reduced Creon to a Kabuki-style villain. The play used multiple Choruses, including a Chorus of the dead, which Polynices, Haemon, and Antigone joined, and a Chorus of Teiresiases, both of which articulated the play's overall point of view. The Chorus of ghosts, for example, sang Sophocles' famous 'Ode on Man' to stress the human inability to control the threat of death. They took apart Antigone's cave to create a structure resembling a lotus flower from which she emerged to join the world of the dead at the western exit. Creon, in dialogue with the Chorus of Teiresiases, rejects their advice, fails to express remorse, and is left alone as the Chorus of the dead, wearing photos of themselves (as at Buddhist shrines to the dead in Japanese homes), moved towards a large pool in front of the museum. They floated illuminated lanterns representing the souls of the dead on the water as in the Japanese obon festival and then joined a procession into the audience.

A version of *Antigone* performed a number of times since 2006 in the Italian Apennines at a German World War II military cemetery holding 30,000 bodies at the Futa Pass by Gianluca Guidotti and Enrica Sangiovanni's Archivio Zeta theatre company also addressed the past, not only through the setting but through special voices developed by the actors to address both the living and the dead, whether enemies or friends. This play's Antigone treated all the dead as deserving to be remembered and loved at a site where Italians fought their former German allies as well as other Italian citizens in a civil war. Many of the victims were never properly identified or buried. Antigone, and often the other actors, spoke many of their lines looking directly at the gravestones rather than at the audience and out to the valley beyond it that sometimes echoed their shouts. All the actors used harsh, loud, anti-naturalistic voices that created a sense of remoteness from the present and included the dead, but Antigone's voice was especially linked with this mode of performance.

This project, originally addressed to local audiences who also participated in the performance, expanded to include broad audiences over time. The audience entered the cemetery and, guided by Chorus and actors, moved slowly up a hill to a funerary monument on a high terrace with one room and a crypt below that served as

Antigone's cave. Creon was confronted not by a live guard but by
an anonymous dead World War II solider who seemed to speak to
his fellow dead as he described Antigone's mourning over her
brother's body, a mourning he had not received. Antigone's first
address to Creon and the Chorus on the terrace was powerful from
the start. She accused the Chorus of cowardice in not facing the
king and provoked a dictatorial anger in Creon. Ismene joined her
sister and Haemon emerged from the audience as the only witness
to speak out among characters and audience. Antigone spoke her
last words from the crypt below the terrace that gave a strange
sound to her voice as she slowly receded into its darkness. The audience was then invited to watch the scene between Creon and Teiresias on the sunny side of the monument. Both actors shouted at each
other from a distance and addressed the tombs of the soldiers.
Teiresias went back down the hill, leaving Creon on his seat of
power until he heard of the deaths of Antigone and his family. The
audience left him silent and alone as they too descended the hill at
the behest of the Chorus-leader and exited from the far side of the
cemetery at sunset.

Sahika Tekhand's version of *Antigone* in Istanbul in 2006,
Eurydice's Cry, addressed issues relating to freedom of expression
and human rights in contemporary Turkey, represented the conflict
of 'voices' in the play through the movement of the actors' bodies.
In this version a Chorus of eight men and women wearing black were
divided into two units of four. Each performer had a spotlight
directed at his or her feet. Actors could only be seen, talk or move
when lit. The voice and movement of the actors was stylized and
limited to a finite number of poses. Movements associated with
Creon were restricted and constrained, sometimes suggesting exag-
gerated or distorted versions of a military pose. Poses associated with
Antigone were stylized, but more fluid, vibrant and emotional, as
well as different for each performer; their hands moved to express
grief or panic. In the beginning of the play the Chorus's movements were associated with the play's repressive leader Creon;
when he was present, all moved in unison. But Antigone's rebel-
lious movements gradually infected Ismene, Haemon, then Chorus members, and Creon's wife Eurydice until Creon was left alone
while the others moved each in their own way in solidarity with
Antigone, although the Chorus continued to speak together.
Emotive sounds emitted by the actors underlined their reactions as
well. The words of the text were spoken faster and faster, but the
direction of the action remained clear through movement. The
play's four episodes were divided by choral odes and moved from
suspicion to fear to pain to rebellion and change. Once the other
actors were aligned with Antigone, Eurydice, who had observed the

action from the beginning, cried out, and, as in Jean Anouilh's French version of the play, broke her Sophoclean silence to scream, speak and curse.

Femi Osofisan's Nigerian *Tegonni: An African Antigone* brings a nineteenth-century Yoruba princess into dialogue with Sophocles' heroine. The play is set under British colonial rule. The first production was staged in Atlanta, Georgia, due to a period of military dictatorship and corruption in Nigeria. The all-black cast staged a romance and disrupted marriage between Tegonni and a young white district officer named Captain Allan Jones. The extraordinarily talented Tegonni had received support from Allan in her quest to become an official bronze caster and member of the guild of carvers, which generally excluded women. Her wedding procession is interrupted by the appearance of the dead body of one of her two brothers, who had been left exposed as a message against rebellion by the Governor, Lt. General Carter-Ross, the adopted father of Allan, who also disapproves of Allan's marriage to a black, African woman. Allan fails to persuade the General to change his mind about the burial and Tegonni is arrested—for burying her brother—along with her devoted female friends, who also serve as a Chorus that frequently performs African song and dance.

Tegonni is offered the chance of release if she officially apologizes for her action. After a series of escapes and further resistance on the part of Tegonni and her friends, she and Allan are eventually shot, the Governor has a heart attack, and the dead Tegonni and her friends reappear on the sacred boat of her patron deity, the water goddess Yemoja. Antigone has come across time to help orchestrate this scenario, and she plays an active role in the plot. In a final dialogue, Antigone tests Tegonni's resolve. Tegonni refuses to apologize to save her life and thus to confirm the subservient status of her people. Antigone finally joins Tegonni on Yemoja's boat. In this play the bonds between the assertive Tegonni, her female friends and her community add a new dimension to the myth, and the play underlines an uneasy correspondence between the story of the Greek Antigone and the African Tegonni.

Among the many versions of *Antigone* chronicled by George Steiner in his book *Antigones*, Bertolt Brecht perhaps offers in his *Antigone* the most critical view of the play's characters. First performed in Chur, Switzerland, in 1948, shortly before Brecht's return to Germany from exile after World War II, the play refused to allow Antigone to represent religious tradition, humanity, the family, the individual in opposition to the state, or opposition to tyranny. For Brecht the play becomes a quarrel among members of a ruling class. The Chorus of Theban elders follows and supports Creon's aggressive imperial war against the Greek city of Argos in order to acquire metals. Polynices is killed for deserting Creon's army after Eteocles dies. The Chorus, thinking the army was victorious, celebrates until they discover that the Theban young men, including Creon's son Megareus, have lost to the Argives and died. Yet the Chorus closes the play still following and collaborating with the failed Creon.

In this version Antigone rebels, but only after Polynices is killed: 'But she who saw everything / could help nobody but the enemy who is now coming and will quickly wipe us out.' At the same time, tied to a board after her capture, Antigone is allowed to speak the play's central point: 'Anyone who uses violence against the enemy will turn and use violence against his own people.' She objects to sacrificing Thebes' young men against peaceful Argos. 'When we forget the past,' she insists to Ismene, 'the past returns'. And once condemned, she strides off to her punishment with a movement suggesting a new freedom. This stride, which was performed as if it made Antigone famous by Brecht's wife Helene Wiegel, nevertheless seems to restore a powerful if flawed voice to Antigone. Yet in Brecht's version of the famous 'Ode on Man,' 'Man counts what is human / as nothing at all. He has become / his own monster.' Human corruption and imperialism rather than fate govern the action of this version of Sophocles' play.

Antigone has become the most performed Western play in a global context, and important productions have appeared in most countries worldwide. The performance of an apolitical *Antigone* seems virtually impossible. As these examples have shown, contemporary relations between family and state, ruler and ruled, or male and female inevitably condition audience responses to performances of the play in translation or in new versions of it. In the USA some productions have tried to avoid suggesting any correspondence between the American President [Donald Trump] and Creon, and have turned to the more sympathetic portrait of Creon in Jean Anouilh's French version of the play * * *, which also makes Antigone confused and far less ethically authoritative than in Sophocles. In other countries, directors have tried to hide behind the canonical status of Sophocles' play in order to make a political statement through its performance in a context where freedom of speech is repressed. In a number of the cases discussed above, Creon has simply become a villain in contrast to an unambivalently heroic Antigone. In Sophocles' original, however, representation of each character's individual voice remains complex and continues to provoke both philosophical controversy and varied versions and performances.

Sophocles: A Chronology

Sophocles' long life coincided with the emergence of Athens as the political and cultural leader of the Greek world, and he appears to have been enviably prosperous. As an ancient biographer put it, "He was illustrious both in life and in poetry; he was well educated and raised in comfortable circumstances; and he was chosen for political offices and embassies."

Sophocles produced over 120 plays, of which only seven survive, although we have titles and brief quotations from some others. Only two of the surviving plays (*Philoctetes* and *Oedipus at Colonus*) can be reliably dated. His plays were outstandingly successful: he won first prize at the Great Dionysia Festival eighteen times (with seventy-two plays in groups of four, three tragedies and a satyr play); he also won first prize in other festivals and never came lower than second.

496?	Sophocles born in the Athenian suburb of Colonus; his father, Sophilus, may have been a manufacturer of armor.
480	Led the group of boys who performed a *paean* (ritual dance of thanksgiving) in honor of the Athenian victory over the Persians at the Battle of Marathon.
479	End of the Greco-Persian War.
468	First entry in the competition at the Great Dionysia, in which he was victorious over Aeschylus.
440s	Likely time of composition of the earliest surviving plays, *Ajax* and *Antigone*.
443–42	Served as *Hellēnotamias*, one of the financial administrators of the Delian League, the Athens-dominated alliance set up for continued defense against Persia.
441–40	Served as *Stratēgos*, one of the ten elected generals who were the city's top officials, along with Pericles; helped to suppress an attempted revolt from the Delian League by the island of Samos.
431	Outbreak of the Atheno-Peloponnesian War.
420s	Likely time of composition of *Oedipus Tyrannos*.
420	Reportedly provided in his house an altar and shrine for the newly introduced healing god Aesclepius until a

	temple could be built for him; for this he received the religious title of *Dexiōn* (Receiver of the God).
410s	Likely time of composition of *Electra*.
413	Selected as one of ten *Sumbouloi* (Advisors) to deal with the aftermath of Athens' disastrous naval expedition to Sicily in 415–13.
409	*Philoctetes*.
406 or 405	Sophocles' death.
401	*Oedipus at Colonus* posthumously produced by Sophocles' grandson.

Selected Bibliography

• indicates works included or excerpted in this Norton Critical Edition.

On Greek Tragedy

Csapo, Eric, and William J. Slater. *The Context of Ancient Drama*. Ann Arbor: U of Michigan P, 1994.

Easterling, P. E., ed. *The Cambridge Companion to Greek Tragedy*. Cambridge: Cambridge UP, 1997.

Foley, Helene. *Female Acts in Greek Tragedy*. Princeton: Princeton UP, 2001.

Goldhill, Simon. *Reading Greek Tragedy*. Cambridge: Cambridge UP, 1996.

Gregory, Justina, ed. *A Companion to Greek Tragedy*. Malden, MA: Blackwell, 2005.

Hall, Edith, *Greek Tragedy: Suffering Under the Sun*. Oxford: Oxford UP, 2010.

McClure, Laura. *Spoken Like a Woman: Speech and Gender in Athenian Drama*. Princeton: Princeton UP, 1999.

Scodel, Ruth. *An Introduction to Greek Tragedy*. Cambridge: Cambridge UP, 2010.

Taplin, Oliver. *Greek Tragedy in Action*. London: Routledge, 2003 [1978].

On Sophocles

Garvie, A. F. *The Plays of Sophocles*. 2nd ed. London: Bloomsbury, 2016.

Jouanna, Jacques. *The Plays of Sophocles: A Study of His Theater in Its Social and Political Context*. Princeton: Princeton UP, 2018.

Markantonatos, Andreas, ed. *Brill's Companion to Sophocles*. Leiden: Brill, 2012.

Morwood, James. *The Tragedies of Sophocles*. Bristol: Bristol Phoenix Press, 2008.

Ormand, Kirk, ed. *A Companion to Sophocles*. Malden, MA: Wiley-Blackwell, 2012.

• ———. *Exchange and the Maiden: Marriage in Sophoclean Tragedy*. Austin: U of Texas P, 1999.

• Segal, Charles. *Sophocles' Tragic World*. Cambridge, MA: Harvard UP, 1995.

On Antigone

Bennett, Larry J., and Wm. Blake Tyrrell. "Sophocles' *Antigone* and Funeral Oratory." *American Journal of Philology* 111 (1990): 441–56.

• Butler, Judith. *Antigone's Claim: Kinship Between Life and Death*. New York: Columbia UP, 2000.

Cairns, Douglas, ed. *Sophocles: Antigone*. London: Bloomsbury, 2016.

Cropp, Martin. "Antigone's Final Speech (Sophocles, *Antigone* 891–928)." *Greece & Rome* 44 (1997): 137–40.

Foley, Helene P. "Sacrifical Virgins: Antigone as Moral Agent." In *Female Acts in Greek Tragedy*. Princeton: Princeton UP, 2001. 172–200.

———. "Tragedy and Democratic Ideology: The Case of Sophocles' *Antigone*." In *Tragedy, History, Theory: Dialogues on Athenian Drama*, ed. Barbara Goff. Austin: U of Texas P, 1995. 131–50.

Goheen, Robert. *The Imagery of Sophocles' Antigone*. Princeton: Princeton UP, 1951.

Goldhill, Simon. "Antigone and the Politics of Sisterhood." In *Laughing with Medusa: Classical Myth and Feminist Thought*, ed. Vanda Zajko and Miriam Leonard. Oxford: Oxford UP, 2006. 141–61.

• Griffith, Mark. "Antigone and Her Sister(s): Embodying Women in Greek Tragedy." In *Making Silence Speak: Women's Voices in Greek Literature and Society*, ed. André Lardinois and Laura McClure. Princeton, Princeton UP, 2018. 117–36.

Griffith, Mark, ed. *Sophocles: Antigone*. Cambridge: Cambridge UP, 1999.

Harris, Edward M. "Antigone the Lawyer, or the Ambiguities of *Nomos*." In *Law and the Courts in Ancient Greece,* ed. Edward M. Harris and Lene Rubinstein. London: Bloomsbury, 2004. 19–56.

Kitzinger, Rachel. *The Choruses of Sophokles' Antigone and Philoktetes: A Dance of Words*. Leiden: Brill, 2008.

Murnaghan, Sheila. "*Antigone* 904–920 and the Institution of Marriage." *American Journal of Philology* 107 (1986): 192–207.

Neuberg, Matt. "How Like a Woman: Antigone's Inconsistency." *Classical Quarterly* 40 (1990): 54–76.

Oudemans, Th. C. W., and André Lardinois. *Tragic Ambiguity: Anthropology, Philosophy and Sophocles' Antigone*. Leiden: Brill, 1987.

Roisivach, Vincent. "On Creon, Antigone, and Not Burying the Dead." *Rheinisches Museum* 126 (1983): 192–211.

Sourvinou-Inwood, Christiane, "Assumptions and the Creation of Meaning: Reading Sophocles' *Antigone*." *Journal of Hellenic Studies* 109 (1989): 134–48.

———. "Sophocles' Antigone as a 'Bad Woman.'" In *Writing Women into History*, ed. Fia Dieteren and Els Kloek. Amsterdam: U of Amsterdam, 1990. 11–38.

• Stuttard, David, ed. *Looking at Antigone*. London: Bloomsbury Academic, 2018.

On the Later Reception of Sophocles' Play

Mee, Erin, and Helene P. Foley, eds. *Antigone on the Contemporary World Stage*. Oxford: Oxford UP, 2011.

Miola, Robert S. "Early Modern Antigones: Receptions, Refractions, Replays." *Classical Receptions Journal* 6 (2014): 221–44.

Steiner, George. *Antigones: How the Antigone Legend Has Endured in Western Literature, Art, and Thought*. Oxford: Oxford UP, 1984. Paperback reprint, New Haven: Yale UP, 1996.

• Wilmer, S. E., and Audronė Žukauskaitė, eds. *Interrogating Antigone in Postmodern Philosophy and Criticism*. Oxford: Oxford UP, 2010.